CDO
CHIEF DADDY OFFICER

CDO
CHIEF DADDY OFFICER
The BUSINESS of FATHERHOOD

CHRISTOS EFESSIOU

WITH CONTRIBUTIONS BY PERSEPHONE EFESSIOU

Advantage®

Leading Expert Testimonials

"CDO Chief Daddy Officer *is a very personal account of the journey and adventure of parenting, using the fundamental business skills of effective communication, team building and managing time. It offers personal tips and advice as well as universal parenting wisdom to inspire you to be the best parent you can be.*"
—SUE ATKINS, Author, Speaker, BBC Broadcaster

"*I love this book! All of Chris' strategies mirror my own advice to parents and caregivers with children of any age. By approaching the tasks of managing a household using the same tactics used in business, parents can create their own successful family dynamic. Integrating these strategies with a healthy dose of compassion and love for your children will make all the difference.* CDO Chief Daddy Officer *is solid proof! A magnificent book for all parents who wish to build lasting relationships with their sons and daughters.*"
—MARIA BAILEY, CEO BSM Media, Author, Host of *Mom Talk Radio* and MomTV.com

"*This book was at the same time instructive and inspirational. I salute Chris for the time he has taken to share his wisdom with the reader. I also salute him for his integrity and leadership both in business and in his personal life. I hope this work is the first of more to follow as clearly this is a man of vision, wisdom, energy, integrity and above all LOVE.*"
—JOEL BATZOFIN, MD, Reproductive Endocrinologist

"*This book is* The Guide for Getting an MBA in Parenthood. *It is amazing to me how Chris Efessiou was able to clearly and concisely use the basic principles of business management to produce a manual on being a successful parent. No one said parenthood would be easy, but the principles obtained from this book*

can give all parents the common sense business approach to be a loving, caring mentor to their child. I highly recommend this instruction manual for all parents and parents-to-be, because the most important business is the business of bringing up a child."
—MICHAEL BLAISS, MD, Memphis, TN

"CDO Chief Daddy Officer *is every parent's manual to raise their children to become un-entitled, caring adults. Chris Efessiou eloquently and with a hefty sense of humor outlines the similarities found in all thriving businesses to the journey of raising a self-sufficient and responsible child. Through personal accounts, you will experience the success story of this very special father-daughter relationship and you will rejoice in its triumph of overcoming countless challenges each of which made their bond stronger. I would strongly recommend this book to any parent who wishes to raise a child to become a fine adult."*
—DR. MICHELE BORBA, *TODAY* Show Contributor, Author of 23 Parenting Books

"*Where was* Chief Daddy Officer *when I was raising my daughter by myself? My knowledge of business principles was even less than my knowledge of child rearing. In this book, I got lessons in both. Chris Efessiou gave us an easy-to-read manual on how to raise a well-adjusted, independent, happy adult – one who understands the importance of giving back to the community. This busy, successful CEO practiced what he preached. If you want to succeed at both, business and parenting, this book will be your guide."*
—JAN FOX, 4-Time Emmy Award Winning Broadcaster, Speaker, Coach, Author

"*The most important leadership role we will ever have is at home. It's also often the most challenging. That's why I highly recommend this book! Read it today and let your greatest legacy be the lessons you teach your children by the way you lead them."*
—JON GORDON, Best-Selling Author of *The Energy Bus* and *The Seed*

I found this book to be extremely insightful and well written. I believe it should accompany each car seat upon a newborn's discharge from the nursery.
—**BRADLEY E. CHIPPS**, MD, Sacramento, CA

"*I picked this book up to see if it was worth giving to my son, who is a busy executive with a 2 1/2 year old child. The short answer is yes! This book is full of useful, savvy, worthwhile advice that will be helpful to any parent trying to juggle work and family responsibilities. I particularly liked the way the author kept his priorities straight, while balancing dual challenges. So, yes, I did give this book to my son and will do so to my other children when they too have children. Nothing could be more worthwhile that to succeed at parenting, along with your job.*"
—**MICHAEL KALINER**, MD, Chevy Chase, MD

"*This was a great book and one I would recommend to all fathers. It will help you see work and life as needing complementary and not competing skill sets. And you will never quite see your role as father in the same way again. Read my book review of* CDO Chief Daddy Officer *and then buy or download the e-book for your own library. You will not regret it.*"
—**WAYNE PARKER**, About.com Guide

"*As a Vistage Chair I work closely with 32 CEOs and their senior executives every month. Having read Chris' book I am eagerly recommending it to my Vistage members. I believe the book is in alignment with the mission of Vistage, which is "Dedicated to Increasing the Effectiveness and Enhancing the Lives of Chief Executives." The book is a great reference guide with respect to how to leverage the experience and expertise gained on the job to more effectively raise our children. It is an easy read full of real life examples that will bring smiles to your faces and tears to your eyes. This book will provide perspective as well as useful tips on how to handle difficult conversations, accountability, and the tough decisions that are coming.*"
—**PETER SCHWARTZ**, Chair-Vistage International

"This book is loaded with practical lessons in personal growth, leadership and parenting. His entertaining stories will motivate you to be a better parent, leader and role model. I would recommend this book to all parents, CEOs, employees and college students entering the work force. You will be touched by this book – a truly great book!"
—GORDON J. BERNHARDT, CPA, PFS, CFP®, AIF®, President & CEO, Bernhardt Wealth Management, Inc.

"CDO is a thoughtful application of foundational business wisdom to the practice of parenting. It is eminently sensible in both HOW business fundamentals could be applied to parenting, but also WHICH business fundamentals should be applied. It resonated with me as an academic, but also with me as a father; it uses business principles legitimately but explains them in a genuinely warm and accessible way. I would recommend it to anyone on the journey that is parenting."
—MATTHEW A. CRONIN, PhD, School of Management, George Mason University

This book is a how-to book on raising children. For the first time we now have some superb practical advice on now to 'mentor' our children in the same manner that we would mentor someone in the business world. The author has taken the unique approach of using good business principles and applying these to raising children. We can learn a lot from the real-life examples in the book which are used to show us the application of these principles. I would suggest this book for any and all parents.
—WILLIAM STORMS, MD, Colorado Springs, CO

Advantage Media Group is proud to be a part of the Tree Neutral® program. Tree Neutral offsets the number of trees consumed in the production and printing of this book by taking proactive steps such as planting trees in direct proportion to the number of trees used to print books. To learn more about Tree Neutral, please visit www.treeneutral.com. To learn more about Advantage's commitment to being a responsible steward of the environment, please visit www.advantagefamily.com/green

Advantage Media Group is a leading publisher of business, motivation, and self-help authors. Do you have a manuscript or book idea that you would like to have considered for publication? Please visit www.amgbook.com or call 1.866.775.1696

Dedication

To Persephone, my mother,
for the unconditional love and support
she has given abundantly to her three children
and for allowing me to observe in her
the essence of parenting.

To Persephone, my daughter,
for respecting me as her father and for
loving and honoring me as her dad.

To Juliana for being Juliana.

"Love, Laugh, Live and Give."

– Quincy Jones

Table of Contents

*"This is, in essence,
the book I wish I had had when
I embarked on this journey."*

Introduction

WHEN MY DAUGHTER WAS JUST 3 YEARS OLD, *Fortune* ran a cover story titled "Why Grade 'A' Execs Get an 'F' as Parents." At the time I was rising quickly through the ranks of a pharmaceutical company, and I was already well aware that I was surrounded by workaholics. My coworkers and superiors arrived at the office early and left late. A glance through this article seemed to confirm my worst fears, lamenting that, "For all their brains and competence, powerful, successful executives and professionals often have more trouble raising kids than all but the very poor."[1]

I pored over the paragraphs with great interest, quickly finding their contents depressing. More than a third of high-powered executives' children at one company had been treated for psychological or drug abuse problems; many such children were packed off to boarding schools. The author interviewed experts who listed warning signs for depression and suicide so that concerned parents could intervene before the unthinkable happened. The theme of the article seemed to be that the qualities that make a successful executive make for a neglectful, insensitive parent. That night, as I tucked my daughter into bed, I vowed silently that I would never become one of those parents.

Five short years later, my vow was put to an unexpected test. The success I had found in my professional life had not been matched in my marriage. The divorce was ugly, but it was the only way out of an even uglier situation. My daughter decided that she wanted to live with me, rather than move away with her mother. The three of us agreed. So in a

[1] Brian O'Reilly and Sarah Hammes, "Why Grade 'A' Execs Get an 'F' as Parents," *Fortune*, January 1, 1990.

flash I became a single father and a rising executive, perhaps the perfect recipe for every catastrophe warned of in that article.

I am grateful to say I was able to keep my vow. My daughter is, at this writing, a lovely, successful young woman in her early 20s, and we share a relationship more wonderful than I could have ever dreamed. What I discovered on my journey to this place, ironically, was that one of the fundamental propositions of that *Fortune* article was wrong, or at least it was wrong for me. I found that the very same qualities and techniques that enabled me to succeed in business also enabled me to succeed as a father.

When I stared across the dining room table at my 7-year-old daughter nearly 17 years ago, I had no idea what I was doing. If my life had been a movie, this would have been the point that we eschewed bedtime, ate chocolate sundaes for breakfast, and generally lived life as a slumber party until I realized that's no way to raise a child. But this was real life, and not knowing what you're doing in real life is a real problem. So I thought for a long time about what I knew how to do well. What was I good at? I was good at my job. The next two questions were trickier: What had enabled me to be successful at my job? How could I transfer that success to the goal of raising my daughter to be a happy, well-adjusted and successful adult?

I began to develop a series of principles and strategies that I would test and revise in the years that followed. Because I was drawing on my business experience, I knew that I would make mistakes. But I also knew those mistakes didn't have to be devastating; I could avoid the destructive blunders and learn from the rest. And this is precisely what happened. I learned that the same dedication and determination that built my business could help my daughter navigate adolescence. The same encouragement that brought out the best in my employees would make sure that homework got done. Over and over, I was shocked by how seamlessly and successfully these principles could be translated from work to home.

I wrote this book, at the urging of my daughter and Juliana, my wife of the last two years, to encourage and inspire parents who find themselves in the same situation I was in. This is, in essence, the book I wish I had had when I embarked on this journey. While not everyone is a single parent as I was, countless parents find themselves in demanding careers and are driven to succeed. I want those parents to know that the very efforts that enable them to be successful at work can be invested simultaneously at home.

Mom and Dad are already working hard to develop the skills needed for their careers; I want to inspire and urge them to apply those skills to their greatest investment of all: their children.

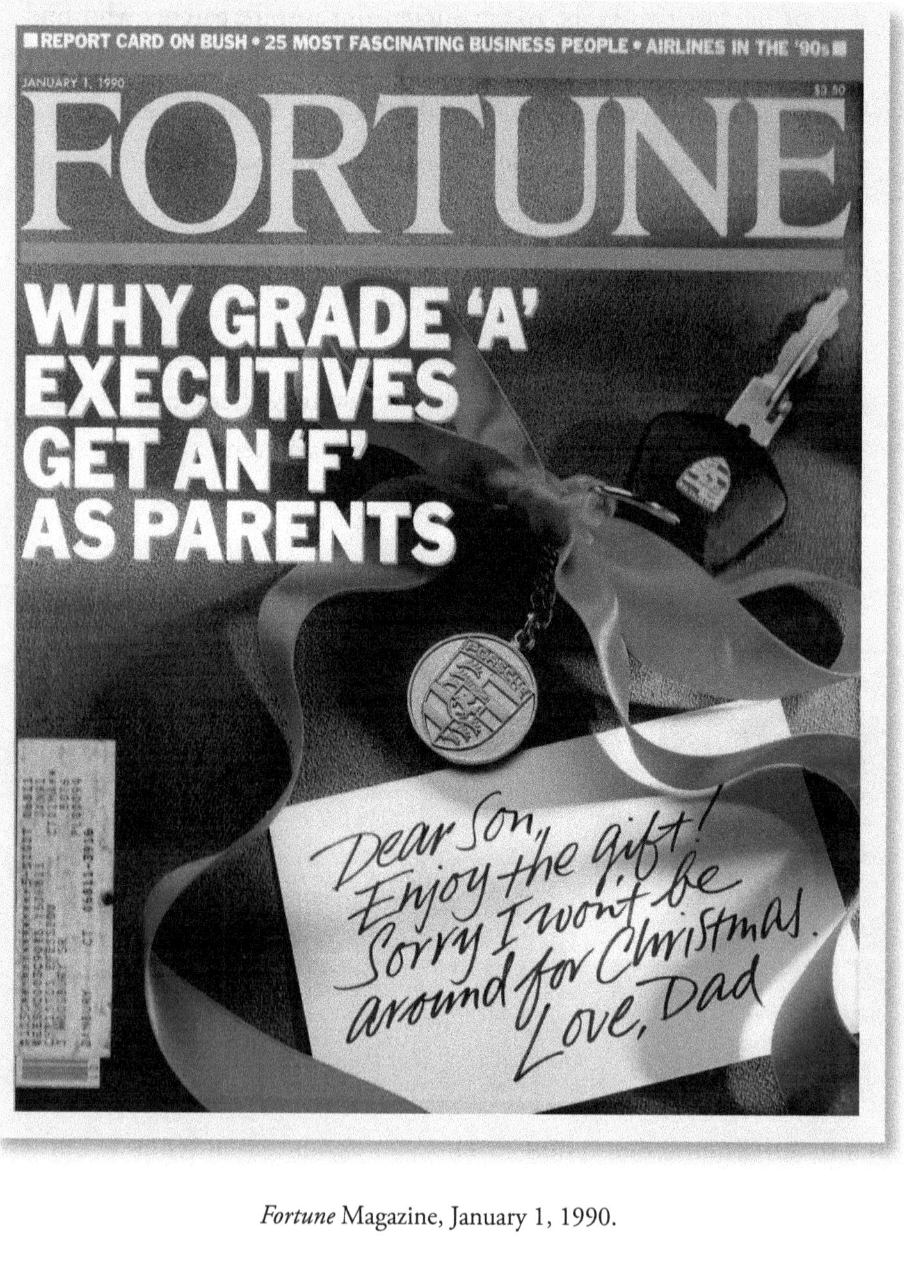

Fortune Magazine, January 1, 1990.

Part I

The
BIG PICTURE

"I think that the unpredictable aspects of parenthood – just like the marketplace – make our planning and preparation all the more crucial."

CHAPTER 1

WHERE ARE WE GOING?

SEVERAL MONTHS BEFORE MY DAUGHTER WAS BORN, I received a copy of Bill Cosby's *Fatherhood* for Christmas. To this day, it has influenced my philosophy of parenting more than any other book. Part humorous masterpiece and part memoir, Cosby's book spoke directly to my situation. True, he was a married entertainer raising five children, and I was a divorced businessman raising one. But we were of roughly the same generation. His account of the well-meaning but authoritarian method employed by his parents reminded me of my own childhood, even though I was raised an ocean away.

Fatherhood showed me that there was a path from my own upbringing—which had many positive as well as some negative aspects—to the kind of life I wanted to provide for my daughter. It showed what one can accomplish armed with just common sense and a hefty dose of humor. Most important, it got me thinking proactively about the kind of father I wanted to be and what kind of results I was looking for.

Imagine starting a business with only a vague idea of what kind of product you will sell. "Oh, I don't know," you tell your potential investors. "Maybe we'll market cell phones in South America, or maybe we'll groom poodles in Manhattan. We'll just wait and see how it goes." Obviously, this scenario is ridiculous. You never start a business without a clearly defined plan and a set of goals. Yet most of us begin parenting with only a vague idea of where the process is headed, treating childhood almost as a permanent state instead of a transitional phase to adulthood. After reading *Fatherhood*, I asked myself three questions:

- What are my goals as a father?
- Do I have what it takes to reach those goals?
- How will I know when I've achieved them?

Much of parenting is unavoidably spontaneous: You don't know ahead of time which night you'll be awake with a sick child or when you'll have to stop what you're doing to get gum out of her hair. So when I say that I put a lot of thought into even the timing of having a child, I don't mean to imply that everything about my parenting was calculated. However, I think that the unpredictable aspects of parenthood – just like the marketplace – make our planning and preparation all the more crucial.

"What is our goal? How well-equipped are we to reach that goal? How will we measure success? Answering these questions is just as important to the success of your parenting as it is to the success of your company."

Asking the Right Questions

By the time Persephone made the decision to live with me, I had asked myself very similar questions about my business endeavors, answered them effectively, and reached my goals. This gave me confidence that I could achieve the same results with my daughter. Sure, the details were different: character qualities in place of profits and healthy self-esteem instead of market share. But the process of planning, execution and evaluation were very similar.

The questions are basic: What is our goal? How well-equipped are we to reach that goal? How will we measure success? Answering these questions is just as important to the success of your parenting as it is to the success of your company.

All parents can feel overwhelmed by what we can't control. When you first hold that tiny, helpless human being in your arms, you are focused solely on keeping her warm, safe and well-fed. Yet at some point during those early years of diapers and midnight feedings you need to ask yourself: What do I want for this child's future?

High-achieving parents can easily run into trouble when asking these questions. It's so easy for us to move from the realm of prudent planning to self-indulgent fantasy. We want a child whose IQ is off the charts, who wins every possible award at her school, plays her instrument in Carnegie Hall at the age of 10, and goes to the Olympics in the sport of her choice. These kinds of goals would be comparable to saying you will take 90% of the market share in an industry during your company's first three weeks in existence: It's a nice thought, but it's probably not going to happen.

No parent can build a child to order, but we can certainly influence who he or she becomes. So after we account for all the factors we cannot control – inborn ability levels and so on – we must ask ourselves whom we want them to become. I will posit that every mentally sound parent wants to raise a healthy, happy child who grows up to be a responsible and productive adult. That is the goal I arrived at when I asked myself the key parenting questions, and it guided all my decisions as a father.

In business, we have very concrete ways of evaluating how well-equipped we are to reach our goals: Do we have the knowledge, the finances, the manufacturing capacity? Similarly, parents must ask themselves if they have the qualities and resources they need to raise their children. Just as a businessman takes inventory in his warehouse, parents need to take stock of their patience, wisdom and capabilities.

Measuring success is trickier. In business, success is usually defined by profitability or at least the reduction or absence of loss. At any given point, you can know the absolute health of your company and exactly how you are performing, and how that compares with the goals of you and your shareholders. The "yardstick" or standard in parenting is much less concrete.

Far too often, parents compare their child with other children, or worse, to themselves. Are you performing at the top of your class? Are you in the most advanced math group? Can you run faster or play your instrument better than anyone else in your peer group? There are several problems with such comparisons. First, our children are unique. Each of them is different from any other person, including their parents. Second, comparisons never bring out the best in anyone, because they subjectively imply that someone else is better. I was constantly compared with other children and I never appreciated it.

Perhaps your child is not a particularly gifted athlete, but works hard to improve. This should be celebrated even if he is not the best in his class. On the other hand, your daughter may be the best violinist in her school but still not living up to her potential because she does not practice enough. Striking the right balance between challenging and encouraging your children requires that you know them as well as you know your job.

"In the United States, the overwhelming majority of children have plenty of food to eat, yet many of them do not have enough time with Mom and Dad."

Kids Today

Too many children do not have a clearly defined standard by which to measure their behavior and performance. For many, the standard is set unrealistically high or shamefully low. When this is the case, the child has no clear path to success because the parents have not been clear or realistic about their goals. Responses can range from frustration to distress.

We all know there are troubled children in the world. News stories and television specials remind us about absentee fathers and failing public schools, children who go to bed hungry or suffer abuse and neglect at the hands of the adults in their lives. We don't hear as much about the problems of children of the middle and upper classes. And why should we? These kids are well-fed, well-educated, and, for the most part, well-supervised. Maybe the warnings I read about in that 1990 *Fortune* article were overblown.

Or maybe not.

The largest shift from the world Bill Cosby and I grew up in to today is the rise in two-career households. I would never argue that this, in and of itself, is a bad thing. Cosby's own wife, Camille, managed his career and later ran a production company and several philanthropies, all while raising their five children. However, this phenomenon combined with the increased hours many men and women are required to work has taken its toll on family life.

Problems such as depression, drug abuse, obesity and even suicide among the children of middle- and upper-class parents provide clues that, despite all our professional success, all is not well. According to the Centers for Disease Control and Prevention (CDC), youth suicide is the third leading cause of death in teenagers nationwide. A growing epidemic of youth and teen obesity is threatening many of our children with lifelong health issues.

Worldwide, children suffer health problems because of inadequate nutrition or medical care. In the United States, the overwhelming majority of children have plenty of food to eat, yet many of them do not have enough time with Mom and Dad. According to the American Academy of Pediatrics, nearly a third of American children and teens are obese.[2] A Texas A&M study found that increased time with parents was key to preventing and fighting obesity in childhood and later in life.[3]

There are other indicators that parents in the professional classes are not quite getting the job done. Since 2000, the number of adults ages 25-39 still living at home with their parents has risen 32%. This was virtually unheard of in my generation. It was perhaps acceptable for a young woman to live at home until she married, but young men were expected to make their way in the world and become independent. Today, many of our children are postponing adulthood well into

[2]"Obesity in Children and Teens," American Academy of Child and Adolescent Psychiatry, 79 (May 2008).

"Parental Time Key In Fight Against Childhood Obesity," *Medical News Today*, August 13, 2006.

their 30s and 40s! If our goals are to raise happy, healthy children who become independent and productive adults, we are going to have to analyze where we are going wrong.

"Part of our job as parents is to create a 'yardstick' or standard that can measure our children's performance against their abilities, not our own fantasies."

Gap Analysis

Since the evaluation of parenting success is so complicated, let's take a more detailed look at the business world to see what we can learn. All well-managed businesses have quarterly and annual goals, typically known as a "forecast." The difference between the forecast and the actual numbers at any given time is the gap: the distance from where you are to where you want to be. To meet your forecast, you need to bridge that gap.

Gap analysis is the process by which we examine the factors causing the difference and determine what we need to do to achieve our goals. It's a useful tool in just about everything that has a set measurement and a set standard. It doesn't have to be complicated: see where you are, see where you want to be, and determine what it takes to get there.

With children, there is no set standard upon which to perform gap analysis. Parents may leave the pediatrician's office gloating that their child is in the 95th percentile for height or rolled over three weeks earlier than the average baby, but the non-physical development of children cannot really be measured by an average or a median.

How, then, can you measure a child's progress? Part of our job as parents is to create a "yardstick" or standard that can measure our children's performance against their abilities, not our own fantasies. The yardstick must also measure character and behavior – self-respect, respect and concern for others, generosity – calibrated by what we consider moral, ethical and just.

Not only must we create this yardstick, we must communicate its existence and calibration to the child. If I expect my daughter to make her bed every morning, I must tell her I expect this. I must then make sure she knows how to do it, showing her if necessary. If I then discover that she is only making her bed two days out of the week, and I want it made every morning, I need to decide what it will take to make up the "gap." Would it be more effective to punish her for failing to do what I ask or to provide a goal incentive if she does it for an agreed period of time? This is gap analysis in parenting.

"Every parenting strategy is a risk; there is always the chance the child won't respond the way that you hope, but that is a risk you must take!"

Making Adjustments

After analyzing "gaps" in our parenting, we need to be willing to make adjustments to our strategies. It is incredibly challenging to raise children today. The world is full of destructive influences competing for our kids' attention. Most of us, however, have already braved one of the most unforgiving places on earth: the marketplace.

Business is brutal. The market is constantly changing, and if you are unable to adjust, you will find yourself losing money or closing up shop. Successful businesses take calculated risks, evaluate themselves constantly, and make adjustments accordingly. I learned during my first years as Persephone's dad that these kinds of risks and adjustments are vital in parenting as well.

Unfortunately, it is very easy as a parent to try to avoid any kind of danger at all costs. Just as no business will grow without risk, sheltering children too much can make them timid and fearful. They will never learn to ride a bike if Mom and Dad aren't willing to let them skin a knee once in a while, and neither will they make any lasting friendships if we are not willing to let them get their feelings hurt occasionally. In fact every parenting strategy is a risk; there is always the chance the child won't respond the way that you hope, but that is a risk you must take!

When Persephone was about 5, she and her mother fought nearly every morning about what she would wear to school. Persephone was not asking to wear clothes that didn't match or were inappropriate for the weather or the occasion. Yet her mother insisted on picking her clothes every day, leading to much shouting and tears.

I looked at our parenting strategy and realized that it wasn't working. I considered what we might do differently. "Why don't you just give her a limited number of outfits that you find appropriate, and let her pick one?" I suggested to her mom. "You could put them all in one drawer so she could go through that drawer and make her choice." We tried that, and all of a sudden Persephone was excited about what she would be wearing that day. I have known other parents who find similar success with picky eaters, allowing the children to participate in menu planning ahead of time.

Each year, hundreds of businesses close because they are unwilling or unable to adjust to the changing market conditions. I'm fairly certain that many more parents have repeated frustrating arguments with their children because they are unwilling or afraid to evaluate their behavior patterns and make adjustments. Admitting that something isn't working doesn't make you a failure as a parent: It sets you up for success.

Throughout this book, I will invite you to share the memories of my many parenting calculated risks, evaluations, and adjustments. My hope is that you will be inspired and realize that you can to do the same in your own life. I am confident that you will find that the strategies and principles that have made you successful at work can also make you successful at home.

CHAPTER 2

MAKING A PLAN

EVERY SUCCESSFUL BUSINESS STARTS WITH A PLAN, but for some reason we parents have been led to believe that it should all come naturally. Luckily, I was one of those sentimental fathers who began building a relationship with my child while she was still in the womb.

> *"Being professionally ambitious and being a loving and emotionally available parent are not mutually exclusive, because one costs the other absolutely nothing."*

It may be difficult to picture Donald Trump snuggling a newborn or Bill Gates playing catch in the yard, but I do hope they took the time to do just that. Too many men have long assumed that displays of affection weaken their ability to succeed in professions that require steely determination. I have proven, if to no one else but myself, that possessing a drive to excel in business does not mean one cannot have a loving and affectionate relationship with one's children. Being professionally ambitious and being a loving and emotionally available parent are not mutually exclusive, because one costs the other absolutely nothing.

Like a business plan, your strategy for parenting will need to be flexible. Reality always intervenes and when it does, you will need to make those adjustments we mentioned in the last chapter. Start with your desired endpoint – your goals – and work backward. How will you shape your child into the adult you want him to be? How will you take advantage of the opportunities to guide her development while allowing her to grow into her own person? As you ponder these elements, remember that your parenting plan will serve as a starting point, not an end in itself. It should be your floor, not your ceiling.

"One of the most challenging experiences for any child is to cope with being different. A child's need to fit in exists in obvious tension with their originality."

Teaching the Impossible

A plan for business or child-rearing must take into account the realities of the marketplace and human nature. You cannot make a business plan that involves an impossible manufacturing process, and you cannot make a plan to rear a healthy adult without factoring in how children actually learn.

I knew one of my greatest tasks as a father was instilling strong character, an open mind, and self-confidence in my daughter. But teaching a child character and other virtues can feel impossible. How do you cultivate qualities in a child that feel difficult to develop in yourself? Yet when I reflected on my experiences at work, I found courage. After all, good bosses must cultivate patience and a strong work ethic in their employees, even if they still struggle in these areas themselves.

Just as employees take their cues from their leaders, I learned that children will imitate, imitate, imitate. I found that the more I made conscious efforts to demonstrate patience, the more Persephone learned to be patient, too. When I took something seriously, so did she. When I laughed something off, she learned that it wasn't that big a deal. This doesn't mean children will always have the same personality as their parents, but it does mean they will gain many of our traits by osmosis.

One of the most challenging experiences for any child is to cope with being different. A childs need to fit in exists in obvious tension with their originality. Indeed, children who are insecure in their uniqueness often face challenges with bullying peers at school. Rather than sitting down with Persephone and reciting a sermon on "just being herself," she learned to embrace her uniqueness with confidence and a sense of humor by watching me.

As an immigrant learning English as a second language, I was immediately recognized as an outsider by my accent. People made fun of me, both jovially and rudely. However, I learned to handle this challenge with self-deprecating humor. I would joke about it when speaking in public and never reacted in humiliation or embarrassment, even though inside it bothered me. I learned that Persephone absorbed my reactions as much as my instructions.

Mentoring and Map-Reading

No one is omniscient. As Persephone grew, I was tremendously relieved to realize that my job wasn't to know everything, but simply to teach my daughter what she needed to know. I wasn't her all-knowing messiah. I was her father and in a practical, but very real sense, her mentor.

"A mentor doesn't dictate how to get to the destination but instead helps to read the map and delineates the waypoints on the charted course."

There is a tremendous difference between mentoring and other kinds of leadership. Those in my dad's generation approached parenting like a dictatorship: What I say goes. It is certainly true that any organization needs authority and structure, and a family is no exception. I discovered, however, that authority does not need to be expressed in a dictatorial fashion. If we keep our goals in mind – raising emotionally healthy, responsible, un-entitled, functional adults – we see that the best approach to parenting is hands-on, deeply involved mentorship.

Mentorship is an ancient art. In earlier generations, young apprentices would be mentored by skilled craftsmen to learn a trade. They arrived eager to learn and left with the skills, expertise and experience to make a living. Children arrive in the world like sponges, ready absorb everything we say and do. Our goal is for them to absorb the information and skills needed to care for themselves and make the world a better place.

A mentor's job isn't to boss people around; it is to pass on knowledge, skills and experience, and guide his people to the desired outcome. Put another way, a mentor doesn't dictate how to get to the destination but instead helps to read the map and delineates the waypoints on the charted course. The mentor knows the terrain and is a good guide in times of uncertainty.

We ultimately want to guide our children on their journey, not travel it for them. At the very beginning, of course, we literally feed and clothe them and care for every one of their needs. Some parents find this a tedious stage, because it is so labor-intensive. I was lucky enough to enjoy it. I loved not just playing with Persephone when she was little, but taking care of her needs: feeding her a jar of baby food or changing her diaper, reading a book to her or later helping her with homework. There is something so precious about the time when children are completely dependent on us, if for no other reason than that it is over so quickly. In the end, the parenting process is about guiding and supporting our children on the journey from dependence to independence.

In business we must cope with the reality of limited resources and prioritize what gets our time, attention and funds. As mentors to our children, we need to decide which values and skills are most important to us. If we want our children to be respectful and polite, we need to begin to monitor those behaviors early in their development. The same goes for being hardworking, responsible and kind.

As we set our priorities, we must keep in mind how children learn. They learn by watching us, not just listening to us. The way you react is how your child will learn to react. By both example and explanation, I was able to teach Persephone that it is OK to laugh at yourself. This was important to me, because I knew that it would help her demonstrate a confidence and comfort in herself that will last her for life.

"Taking the time to answer their questions lets them know we value their curiosity, that we want them to seek our knowledge and advice."

Cultivating Curiosity

One of the qualities I wanted to encourage early on in her development was curiosity. While curiosity in the toddler years can be irritating or even dangerous, that does not mean we should suppress it. I learned this during that wonderful stage known as the "terrible twos." Increased toddler self-awareness often comes across as defiance, but I realized that much of Persephone's mischievousness was actually driven by curiosity.

As she grew and began to find her voice, I was delighted that Persephone was so engaged with the world around her. She was always asking me, "Why?" about nearly everything. Now, this can be quite annoying to a busy parent, but I was lucky enough to remember how my own father took the time to explain the answers to my "whys" when I was young.

I tended to ask rather abstract questions as a child, such as "Why does a boat float while a pin sinks?" "Why do stars not fall from the sky?" "How do airplanes fly?" Persephone asked much more concrete questions: "Why do you need to put gas in the car?" "Why do you have to go to work every day?" "Would you ever do your job for free just because you loved it?"

This showed me that our uniqueness as individuals begins at a very early age. I wanted to take the time to answer her questions as my father had tried to do for me, but also answer them in ways that would be meaningful to her unique perspective. All this was because I valued her curiosity and knew that if properly cultivated, it would serve her well throughout her life.

Her mother's answer to Persephone's "whys" was "Because I told you so," or "Because I'm the mother," or my personal favorite, "Ask your father." Now, we don't have to go overboard and give an answer to the "why" in a way that is over our children's heads. Your 3-year-old probably isn't ready to hear how an internal combustion engine works, but you can tell her that gasoline is like food for the car. Taking the time to answer their questions lets them know we value their curiosity, that we *want* them to seek our knowledge and advice.

The answers will change as they grow. Persephone might ask, "Why do we have to go to church today?" When she was 3, I would tell her, "Because it's Sunday and we go to church every Sunday." When she was 6, I might answer, "Because we need to take time each week to give thanks for what we have been given and to pray for our health and happiness."

In business, employees must feel comfortable approaching their bosses with questions about how to do their jobs or why things need to be done a certain way. An employee who doesn't understand the rationale for a particular HR protocol may end up costing the company a lawsuit. In the same way, if children don't eventually learn the reasons for the rules we give them, they will have no reason to follow those guidelines outside of our presence. More than that, we want our kids to become adults who look for reasons, purpose and principles rather than people who blindly follow whoever happens to be in charge.

Like most things, leadership and cognitive thinking begin at birth and originate at home. Fostering a sense of curiosity allows you a wonderful opportunity to influence your child. You have a chance to share your knowledge in the form of instruction instead of correction, so that it can be considered, adapted, acted upon. That's increasingly important as a child grows. In the early years, parents can control nearly every influence, whether it is television, music, Internet access, or even the friends with whom they play. Later, they will be exposed to all sorts of things, and you want them to come to you when they have questions.

Saying "Because I told you so," too many times is like saying, "Ask someone else" or "Find out some other way." It is a fact of life that children will then ask someone else or find out another way, and at that point you will have lost your opportunity to influence your child. Worse yet, you will have no way of judging the validity of that information, or correcting misinformation.

The Elements of Style

Your style of parenting does not have to dictate its quality. When devising the blueprint for getting your child to adulthood, think of your style as the difference between walking, jogging, or running along the way. The journey's success is determined by whether you reach your destination, not the mode you use to get there.

The same is true in business: There are many roads to profitability and many leadership styles to build a functional team. Obviously, basic ethical boundaries apply, but the details can be all your own. When planning for your child's growth, it is important to be aware of your parenting style, its source, and how it will affect your journey.

"I learned to find ways to reach my goals, even if none were obvious or readily available to me. I learned to imagine solutions to the problem at hand, and then consciously find or engineer a way to make my dream a reality."

Our own upbringing and experiences shape the way we think about parenting. In 1976, when I came to America, I was just shy of my 19th birthday. I had been very vocal about my plans to go abroad. My father, the ultimate negotiator, agreed to make this possible, but with conditions. He made it clear he would send me abroad for a year, but that if I were not in college within that time frame, I would return to Greece and work in his business. If I had taken the latter course, I would have enjoyed a secure yet dishearteningly dependent future, devoid of the opportunity to shape the direction of my own life.

As the first son in a Greek family, I was given privileges, but also a significant number of responsibilities. Our culture held fast to the idea that "To whom much is given, much is expected." I understood that my trip to America was my privilege and that getting into college and graduating were my responsibilities. After managing a multitude of challenges, not the least of which was complete ignorance of the English language, I came to truly realize that nothing is impossible. This was by far my most prized accomplishment up to that point.

After that success, pursuing major challenges became a way of life, personally and professionally. I wanted to do things that had not been done before. I was, in a way, following in my father's footsteps; in another, I was blazing my own trail. Two years later, when I announced that I would be staying in the United States forever, my father wasn't terribly happy with me. Nevertheless, to his credit, he balanced the desire to have me close to home against my arguments for making this country my new home and reluctantly accepted my wishes.

> **"I understood that being smart wasn't enough—to share knowledge, you must be able to communicate clearly."**

Why the change of heart? I'd had an epiphany. I knew that if I returned to Greece, I would never be able to recoup the investment I had made in my future. Many of my classmates who had gone overseas to study had returned to Greece and started their professional lives in the comfort of familiar surroundings and support systems. Inevitably, one of two things happened. Either they quickly became unhappy and settled for something that was not exactly what they wanted, or they left the country again. My gut told me that I had worked too hard to get where I was, and I could not imagine following the same path.

Though I didn't realize it at the time, all these experiences shaped the person and parent I became. I learned to find ways to reach my goals, even if none were obvious or readily available to me. I learned to imagine solutions to the problem at hand, and then consciously find or engineer a way to make my dream a reality.

My first goal was to learn English, and my plan was to learn it from my host family, who happened to be third-generation Greek-Americans. To my dismay, they had their own plan for me, and it did not include speaking English. They thought it appropriate that in exchange for their hospitality, I should teach their children Greek! At a loss, I tried learning from television, but could never reliably discern which accent was correct. Was it *Bonanza, Happy Days, MASH*, or *The Beverly Hillbillies*?

Suddenly, I saw the solution. My host family had two young children, ages 3 and 5, who liked to watch *Sesame Street* on television, and therein lay the answer. I sat with them and listened: The characters spoke slowly and clearly, with structured syllables. For the first time, I could grasp spellings and pronunciations. From there I realized that newscasters were trained to speak proper English, and learned how to differentiate standard English from regional dialects.

I understood that being smart wasn't enough–to share knowledge, you must be able to communicate clearly. From the newscasters, I learned that one also has to look the part, and I started to pick up elements of individuality and style. I had a desire, and later developed an eye, for differentiating myself from others.

One day in the 1980s, while watching the *Today* show, I noticed that Bryant Gumbel was wearing true French cuffs. Years later, as a marketing manager at a major company, French cuffs had become my trademark. Colleagues took note of how I dressed. I did not come to believe that dressing well resulted in good work, but that those who do good work must exhibit quality in everything they do.

These experiences developed in me a tendency to parent in a particular way. I was determined. I would not give in to my child's protests if I knew I was acting in her best interests. However, I also became aware of my need to listen to her and carefully consider her perspective, especially as she got older. So as we make a plan to get from childhood to adulthood in our parenting, we must not only decide which qualities and skills are most important to develop in our children, but also what perspective we bring to the table. These considerations will greatly improve our odds for success!

CHAPTER 3

—✑—

PROACTIVE PARENTING

BUSINESS PUBLICATIONS ARE FULL OF ADVICE on how to lead proactively. Whether you are talking about product development, marketing, management or any number of areas, the question is the same. Will you anticipate what is coming and prepare for it, or will you simply react as things happen?

> *"Too many of us do all our parenting when there is a disagreement or conflict."*

The same question applies to parenting. Much of raising children is necessarily spontaneous. The problem is that too many of us do all our parenting when there is a disagreement or conflict. The only time our kids hear what we expect of them is when they fall short of those expectations. The only time we talk to them about the rules is when they violate them. We react!

Imagine if your current job had no job description. You had no idea what was expected of you and no idea what you could expect of your boss, coworkers or direct reports. You never underwent an orientation, so you had no clue about the policies, procedures, norms or structure of your company. Sounds like a recipe for dysfunction and failure, right? Yet this is precisely what we do to our children when we fail to parent proactively.

Thinking Ahead

People often talk about the difference between playing chess and checkers. Checkers is a simple tactical game; you only need to think a move or two ahead. Chess is a far more complex strategic exercise: a sophisticated strategy can take several moves to implement. It is a game in which you must carefully consider each of your moves as well as your opponent's counter-positions before you take any action.

Parenting is extremely complex. Telling your child that she needs to be good or Santa won't bring her any presents may work in the short term to get her to eat her broccoli. Consider however, what will happen several moves down the road when she realizes Santa is just a fairytale. Does she still have a reason to be good?

Though I had always known the importance of thinking ahead in business, as a father I learned this lesson the hard way. When Persephone's mother and I first separated, I knew she would have lots of questions. But I failed to anticipate how extended time without access to her would affect my daughter and our relationship.

Since I was the one ending the marriage, I was the one who moved out. It seemed only sensible that Persephone and her mother stay in the very comfortable house I had built for us, at least until the divorce was final. I had assumed her mother would share my desire to protect her from the ugly aspects of our breakup. However, a few conversations with my daughter after our initial separation showed me I was very much mistaken.

"Someone is doing voodoo on you, Daddy," she said with uncharacteristic scorn. "You look like Danny Zuko from *Grease*!" she added, referring to the black leather jacket my brother had given me for Christmas. I sensed in her tone of voice that Persephone was distancing herself from me.

At first I was puzzled. Where could she have come up with such ideas? The more I thought about it, the more I realized she was being influenced by people who wanted to drive a wedge between the two of us.

Unfortunately, my worst fears were soon realized. Before I knew it, her mother's lawyer notified me that I was allowed only limited amounts of time with my daughter. I could not see her with regularity, and any time I spent with Persephone was to be the sole decision of her mother, conducted under her terms. Though a "temporary" condition pending other outcomes, it was a crushing blow to my desire and need to spend time with my daughter in the same fashion as I had during the previous eight years of her life. I had been outplayed: I had been playing checkers, while someone else was playing chess. It was not long before I realized I was a few moves away from an unfathomable and unsurvivable outcome: losing my daughter altogether.

I had been blindsided, but the game was not over. I began to strategize and think ahead. If adults were trying to weaken my relationship with my daughter as a weapon in the divorce proceedings, the first thing I needed to do was contend for that relationship. I fought for and received a two-hour visitation slot on Wednesdays, and 48 hours with her every other weekend.

And so a new stage of life began on a road paved with eggshells. I was extremely diligent in maintaining the same parenting style she had come to expect and not make uncharacteristic concessions in an effort to ease the gravity of the situation. I would answer her specific questions about the reasons for the breakup with the same consistent explanation. I would tell her that those reasons were between her parents, and that she was not one of them.

I was committed to never say anything manipulative to my daughter while we were together; I had no interest in her disliking anyone else in her life. I just wanted to ensure we could be close. Within a few months of this increased time together, Persephone told the child psychologist who was helping her through the divorce that she needed more time with me.

What happened during this time was much more than two parents fighting over a child. Through my words and consistent behavior, my daughter saw that I wanted to spend time with her, and that our time together was on the same terms she had always known and could readily identify as ours. I did not become stricter or more lenient with her because of the events around us. I simply wanted to be in her life.

I was not just trying to win the next round of fighting; I wanted to help her with science projects, to read her books, to take her to the same places and do the same things we did before. From that point on, I was determined to do my best to anticipate what lay ahead in my daughter's life and do my best to prepare for the inevitable curve balls, while providing comfort, assurance and consistency.

Words That Encourage

The language we regularly use with our children demonstrates whether we are proactive or reactive parents. How often during the course of the week are we taking the time to instruct our children in an important skill or value? Let's revisit the simple task of making a bed. Suppose your child is 8; you believe this is a reasonable age for him to make his bed on his own, but he fails to do so consistently. How do you speak to him about it? "This bed looks terrible! How could you leave it looking like that?"

"I made sure that the criticisms and corrections I offered her were constructive: no blanket insults, but actionable advice. And I always told her how much I loved her."

While the bed may indeed look terrible, you might ask yourself how much time you have taken to teach your child how to make his bed and to observe him doing it. Have you given him feedback to tell him what he is doing well and what he can do better? I found with Persephone that it was always important to give positive feedback. This meant that I wasn't just correcting the things she did wrong but affirming the things she did right. This strategy goes back to the idea of having a plan. If you have a plan for your child's character and growth, then you want to say encouraging words whenever he does something that fits in the plan. It boosts your child's confidence, fuels his innate desire to please you, and teaches him to recognize opportunities to do the right thing.

I grew up in a generation in which putdowns and insults to one's children were commonplace. "How could you do that?" "This is the worst mess I've ever seen in my life!" "I am embarrassed for you." In my family's case, such insults were never meant maliciously, but that didn't change the fact that they were embarrassing, discouraging and demeaning. They didn't motivate me to work harder; they made me not want to try at all.

When you have been raised with insults and putdowns, it can be very difficult to refrain from using them on your child in a moment of frustration and weakness. I dealt with this problem at home and at work. As someone who fought so hard to learn proper English, I found myself feeling impatient with employees who brought me documents with misspellings or poor grammar.

When Persephone was in high school, I felt similar frustration when she would tell me how hard some of her homework was. I could hear the voice of Bill Cosby in my head, explaining how his father would have to walk miles to school in the snow uphill (both ways!). I fought my urge to say to her, "You were born and educated here. Do you have any idea what it is like to have been in the country for a month and do assignments in U.S. history without knowing the history *or* the language?"

Yet, I knew that if I said such things to her, she would only become discouraged. It would not make her want to work harder; it would make her not want to try at all. Instead, I paid attention to when she was expending more effort and made sure to tell her how proud I was of her. I made sure that the criticisms and corrections I offered her were constructive: no blanket insults, but actionable advice. And I always told her how much I loved her. She always understood, as will your child, that constructive criticism does not mean withholding love and pride in them. It simply provides them with a map, so they know how to navigate the bumps on the road.

Some parents have confused the need to encourage with the idea of getting rid of standards of behavior or performance altogether. This is equally problematic. We have standards for our children's behavior and performance whether we admit it or not. It is NOT OK for a child to curse someone out or to get F's in school. In fact, it is not really OK for a child to be rude or disrespectful and to get A's in school. There is nothing wrong with having these standards. The problem is how we communicate them.

I believe that children are born with a desire to please their parents. It is our job to clearly communicate what they must do to earn our approval. They need boundaries, but the boundaries must be appropriate. If we make them too tight, children will become discouraged and rebel. Expecting a 4-year-old to practice piano two hours a day or a 6-year-old to do algebra is unrealistic. On the other hand, if the boundaries are too wide, children will naturally abuse their freedom. A teenager is fully capable of keeping her room clean and remembering to call when her plans change. If you don't expect this of her, she can quickly get out of hand.

Once you begin to communicate proactively and offer constructive criticism instead of insults, you will never want to go back. The results are so much better: you and your children will grow closer, and they will feel encouraged to try harder at everything they do. If you find yourself in a moment when you are emotionally frustrated with your child, walk out of the room and take a deep breath. Get your feelings under control and go beyond reacting to the situation to asking yourself, "What do I want to come out of this?" Then, with that in mind, go back and speak to your child. I know it may sound easier said than done but it really isn't. It takes some practice and a strong belief in the fact that two wrongs never make a right.

Taking the 30,000-Foot View

Business leaders routinely step back from daily operations to look at the big picture or the "30,000-foot view" in order to effectively guide their organization. Think back to your last flight. You were probably cruising at an altitude of more than 30,000 feet, looking at the world from nearly six miles above sea level. I suspect however, that you were impressed not by how high you were flying, but by how far you could see. The beauty of looking at the big picture is the long and wide view that allows you to see things invisible at ground level.

"The beauty of looking at the big picture is the long and wide view that allows you to see things invisible at ground level."

Parents need similar perspective. They are the managers and leaders of their children, and as such, they, too, will be well-served by taking in the big picture and devising a long-range strategy. It bears repeating: Children become adults. This sounds trite and obvious, but to parent proactively, we must constantly remind ourselves that we are trying to do more than just get through the day. We are raising future adults. What kind of adults do we want them to be?

The old saying goes that you can pick your friends, but you can't pick your relatives. As true as that is, there will come a time in every one of our children's lives when they will be able to choose whether or not they want to have a close relationship with us. When that last check for college tuition has cleared, will they still call for something other than money?

I am grateful that I took the time to think about the adult I wanted Persephone to become. That is not to say I did not face my share of challenges. On several occasions, I had to remind myself that the present difficulties would pass and that Persephone would have many more years of her life as an adult than as a child. So, I set out to parent young Persephone with an eye toward the relationship I dreamed of having with her when she was an adult.

My 50th birthday offered a unique opportunity to catch a glimpse of the results of my parenting efforts thus far. No longer a little girl full of questions, Persephone was a junior in college. I had recently met Juliana, who would become my wife. Our lives seemed to be changing rapidly, and I felt very blessed.

In the midst of these changes, Persephone shared that she really wanted to plan an elaborate birthday party for me. I was deeply touched: how sweet that she even remembered that birthday, let alone wanted to make a big deal about it. She was in college at the time, and she needed my consent for the expenses. I had never dreamed of throwing myself an elaborate event, however I recognized that this was not only very important to her, but also a tremendous learning opportunity.

I asked for a line-item budget to review, but left the details of the planning completely to her discretion. While I had no idea of what to expect, I trusted her judgment completely, and I saw this as my opportunity to watch her fly and show me that she would not fly like Icarus.

When I entered the hotel on the big day, I could not have been more shocked at what awaited me. I was greeted by a very select group of friends and family, including my mother, brother and sister, who had traveled all the way from Greece for the occasion! Persephone had paid meticulous attention to detail, making every choice meaningful.

The terrace overlooked the water, which I love, and the center-pieces featured bamboo, which has always been a favorite plant of mine. Watermelon is my favorite fruit, but was not in season at the time. Yet there were skewers of succulent red watermelon and feta cheese adorning the hors d'oeuvres trays. The cake was in the shape of an airplane – homage to my love of flying – and my initials and "5050" adorned the tail and formed my call sign. The music through the evening was as varied as my taste, from a cellist playing classical music to Usher and Elton John.

But the biggest surprise came during her remarks. Not only did she rise, poised and confident, to speak in front of everyone – this I had come to expect – but her speech centered entirely on how much she valued the way I had raised her. She thanked me for many things, some silly and some serious, but most important to me were these words: "Thank you for helping to guide me through almost 20 years of my life, yet always allowing me to make my own decisions. I pray that one day I will be half the parent you are and continue to be to me."

What a phenomenal tribute! Throughout her childhood, Persephone had, like every child, resisted my views, standards and expectations at various times. Yet here she was, an adult, telling everyone what a good job I had done and expressing the hope that she could do the same for her children. I felt overwhelmed with gratitude. And it was then I realized that my work all those years was to bring us to that place: not that particular moment, but what it represented.

Daddie-

When I first sat down to write this, I found it was a far greater challenge than I could've imagined. I struggled to find the perfect words that could best articulate what I'd like to say, so after much thought I'd like to take advantage of this opportunity to say two simple, yet all encompassing words... "thank you". Thank you for every experience & opportunity that you have given me & that we have shared. Thank you for ~~all your guiding~~ ~~years~~ helping to guide me through almost 20 years of my life yet always allowing me to make my own decisions. Thank you for every morning you woke up to have breakfast with me & to do our dance routine & for every night you waited up for me to come home just so you knew I was safe. Thank you for ~~coming~~ ~~attending~~ never missing a play, dance recital, or any school function ~~ever to ~~~~ever ~~~~~~ever~~~. Thank you for all the nights you tucked me into bed even when I was a senior in highschool. Through both ~~the~~ triumphs & hardships, you have never failed to be the most loving & generous father anyone could dream of. I pray that one day I will be half the parent you are & continue to be me. Happy 50th Birthday Daddy! I love you!

CHAPTER 4

UNDERSTANDING YOUR AUTHORITY

WE HAVE ESTABLISHED SO FAR THAT SUCCESS at work and as a parent are not mutually exclusive. In fact many of the same "best practices" apply both at home and at the office. Let's focus on the very controversial topic of parental authority; this, too, is an area where we can learn much from the marketplace and apply it with our children.

Extreme views of parental authority abound. Those of my parents' generation believed that a parent's word was never to be questioned or discussed. Many parents today believe that it is wrong to ever tell a child "no." The first group of parents believes their strict rules will lead to good behavior, while the second group believes their lack of rules will make their children confident and happy. Unfortunately, both approaches tend to produce undesirable results: *rebellion* in the first case and *chaos* in the second.

So how are we to understand the proper use of our authority as a parent? I don't pretend to have all the answers. However, I can say with confidence that it can be done, and I will share with you the principles and techniques I was able to employ with success.

The Problem of Authority

My own native country of Greece is famous for some of the first experiments with various forms of civil authority. From perhaps the earliest democracy in ancient Athens to the militaristic commune in ancient Sparta, the history of Greece demonstrates that leading others has never been a simple or popular task.

What is the proper way to exercise authority as a parent or as the leader of a company? The answer comes down to balancing needs. Individuals, whether they are employees or children, have the need to think freely, ask questions, and express themselves. The organization, whether it is a company or a family, needs order and cohesiveness. When we are exercising our authority properly, both sides will move toward the center, bending willingly to one another's needs.

A word of caution: Remember that your goal is to create win-win scenarios that benefit both sides. It is easy to lose focus and strive for achieving the elusive "perfect balance" which, if ever achieved, is always extremely unstable and short-lived. When both the leaders of the institution and the individual members learn to consider and accommodate one another, you have a much more sustainable situation.

As the CEO of a company for the last 20 years, I have often struck this balance by relying on my instincts. In retrospect, I realized which principles were guiding my decisions. I may have done the smart thing by nature, but I wasn't always smart enough to realize it! I have always fostered a work environment where all people have a voice and know up front that they will have an opportunity to speak their minds. The ultimate decision, of course, will not be to everyone's liking. Everyone understands, however, that all must comply as if the decision were his or her own and that adherence is not optional.

Over the years, I have dealt with hundreds of employees from a myriad of backgrounds and levels of sophistication, with various personalities. Yet there has been only one occasion in which someone who was unhappy with a final decision tried to undermine it. That was also the single time I had to fire someone in a very public way, creating an example for all to see. I did not enjoy it, but it had to be done. That person had the same opportunity to express an opinion as everyone else and knew my expectations and the consequences. This experience showed me that there are times in life when individuals must experience consequences or the entire organization will come to a halt.

"Allowing people to have a voice empowers them; being decisive empowers the organization."

Although some companies try to solicit opinions through employee satisfaction surveys, I do not believe they work nearly as effectively as personal interaction. Surveys eliminate the possibility for debate – the process by which ideas must be challenged or defended on their merits. Many bosses and managers resist debate because they find it threatening, annoying, or simply an exercise in futility. But in reality, it forces people to stand by their opinions and demonstrate why their way is better. It fosters accountability and responsibility, and gives you the ultimate "vote." Anonymous surveys do not afford employees the opportunity to explain their viewpoint or take responsibility for their proposals.

The older our children grow, the more important it is that they know their voices are heard. I was pleasantly surprised by how willing

Persephone was to go with the option I chose as long as she felt I was giving her viewpoint a fair hearing. At the end of her sophomore year, she informed me that she wanted to work as a hostess at a restaurant near her school. I praised the initiative and asked if she had considered working in an office environment instead of a restaurant. She countered that this was likely to be the "last fun job" she'd have while in school.

I explained that there was nothing wrong with the hostess position, but I wanted her to consider how future employers would weigh an office position versus a restaurant job, particularly since she was majoring in business management. Nevertheless, I left the ball in her court. Initially, she was not thrilled by my raining on her parade, but a few days later she called to tell me that she had opted for the office position, because it was a better move for her career.

When younger children are displeased with a parental decision, let them know it is OK to disagree with you. Maybe your 7-year-old son really wants to see a violent movie with a friend, but you do not think it is a good idea. You can remind him, "I know you are disappointed, son. I even understand why you might be mad, but I am asking you to respect and follow my decision." You will be surprised how often the opportunity to express honest disagreement will satisfy your child and enable him to go along with your decision peacefully.

Teenagers are more likely to need the opportunity to explain why the option they desire is better. Be open to really listen to the merits of their arguments. If it truly is a better option, consider changing your mind. Otherwise, politely acknowledge the good points of what they have said and then restate your decision.

Not too long ago, I had such an experience with Persephone as we began to plan her wedding. I had given her what I thought to be a very generous budget, which seemed sufficient until she fell in love with a venue that was clearly beyond what we had discussed. For a while it seemed her dreams would be shattered if she could not have her wedding there.

I dutifully looked at the information, visited the site, and allowed her to explain to me all of the details that made this place perfect. Then I restated the terms we had agreed to and pointed out that this venue would exceed the budget for the entire wedding. I asked her if she had a plan to come up with the rest of the money she would need. Soon she was able to find another venue that, while it did not appear quite as perfect as the first, was very lovely and within the budget. She saw my reasoning; I soon had a happy bride, and we didn't even have to argue!

The bottom line is this: Let your employees or your children know that their opinions will be heard. Then listen, and seriously consider what they say. After you have given them a fair hearing, come to a decision that provides a win-win outcome and stick to it. Allowing people to have a voice empowers them; being decisive empowers the organization.

Self-Awareness and Consistency

Your credibility will only be as strong as your self-awareness and consistency. You have to understand what motivates you and how you respond, or risk responding irrationally, which will undermine your authority both at home and at work. We will discuss this in more detail in the following chapter on communication, but for now start thinking about the kind of person you are. Specifically, what irritates you most and why?

"Your credibility will only be as strong as your self-awareness and consistency."

Children are experts at pushing our buttons. It is so easy to overreact to their normal antics, and when we do, we lose our children's respect and our ability to manage them. Of course, the same is true at work. A boss whose temper is out of control may command fear but never true respect. The key to staying in control of our responses is to understand what irritates us more than it should.

There are plenty of behaviors that warrant a strong reaction from parents. A child who runs out into the street, steals something from a store, or bites a classmate is demonstrating serious lapses in judgment that need to be addressed swiftly and decisively. A child who is merely whining for more dessert or stalling bedtime is behaving as all children do at times. While the behavior may be irritating, our job isn't to vent our irritation. Our job is to communicate to the child that his specific behavior is not the way to get what he wants.

Take a look in the mirror and ask yourself what your pet peeves are. Is it whining? Disrespect? Sloppiness? Forgetfulness? All these are weaknesses children can learn to overcome, but only if we teach them. If we react to these weaknesses as if our kids were lighting the house on fire, we diminish the effectiveness of our response. They begin to "tune out" everything we say as background noise. Worse yet, they won't take a strong response seriously, even when it is warranted.

We will only achieve our behavior goals with our children if standards are consistently enforced. If whining isn't OK this morning but is overlooked it the afternoon, we are sending mixed signals to our kids. The same is true of any work policy. If the accounting department doesn't consistently review expenditures on travel, no one will take the guidelines seriously. If a teenager gets yelled at for missing curfew one weekend and has it overlooked the next, she will not realistically know what is expected of her, no matter what the "rules" are.

Trust but Verify

Trust is the lifeblood of any relationship. Just as we cannot stand over our employees all day at work, we cannot watch our children every minute of the day. The older they get, the more time they spend out of our direct supervision. This can be very stressful, but it is inevitable, so we must do all we can to cultivate trust. This trust must go both ways. Our children must trust that we will always have their best interests at heart and that we will not lose control of our emotions in a way that will harm them. We must trust them that they will uphold the values we have instilled in them, even outside of our presence.

Perhaps every parent's worst nightmare is the so-called teenage rebellion. Nearly every teen will rebel in some way at some point. Perhaps even you remember resisting your parents' authority at a particular age. We control nearly every influence over young children, but teenagers seem to inhabit an entirely different world. I felt this transition acutely as Persephone entered her teens. Instead of watching my daughter play on the swing set, I was now getting the phone numbers of the people driving her to the movies. I was pleased to see her continue to do well in school, but I could tell she was feeling the effects of peer pressure, like all girls her age. I knew that I had to teach her how to resist the urge to fit in when fitting in would lead her to self-destructive behavior.

"We control nearly every influence over young children, but teenagers seem to inhabit an entirely different world."

As Persephone entered high school, I was surprised at how many of her friends were allowed to arrange their social lives without parental supervision. We would have a friend or two of hers overnight and I would seldom receive a call from their parents verifying their teenager's plans. On the other hand, whenever Persephone went somewhere with a friend, I would always call the parents to verify the arrangements. This would drive her crazy, but my primary concerns were to ensure that she'd be safe, that the plans were indeed what had been communicated to me, and that the other parents were truly comfortable with them. My actions also let my daughter know I would find out if her plans were different from what she had reported.

When Persephone was a freshman, I decided to take a weekend away. She chose to stay in town with her friend Katie. I checked with Katie's mom, and everything seemed to be in order. On my way out, however, I was struck by the fact that her room was uncharacteristically tidy. Noting this, I decided to take another walk through the house. While I was checking around, I noticed that the backdoor was unlocked.

As I pulled out of the driveway pondering these two facts, I grew more and more concerned. I was only a few miles away from the house when I received a call from our housekeeper who reported similar irregularities. I called Persephone on her cell phone and told her I just wanted to check in with her to make sure everything was OK at Katie's house.

"Oh, actually, there's been a change of plans. I'm going to be staying with Ally," she said in a voice that was just a little too eager to please.

At this point, unbeknownst to my daughter, I pulled off the highway, turned around and began heading home. But I answered her casually. "That'll be fine honey. May I have Alley's parents' number, please?"

"Well, I can't really give it to you right now, because I'm going to meet her later."

I continued to ride back to my home and called Persephone a little bit later, only to learn her plans had changed yet again. I put in a call to a mother whose number I did have, and found that she had no idea what was going on with her daughter either. Finally, I arrived back at my home and pulled my car into the garage. As a precaution, I removed our spare key from its hiding place and disabled the keypad access to the garage door. Persephone was effectively locked out of the house. Then I went inside and waited.

About an hour and half later, Persephone arrived in a car with several friends. I watched them from the upstairs window as she tried in vain to enter the house by repeatedly keying the access code to the garage door and looking for the spare key. Then she caught a glimpse of my car in the garage. Panicked, she jumped into the car with her friends, and they sped away.

I immediately called her on her cell phone. She answered with hardly a whisper.

"Persephone, put me on speaker," I demanded calmly. She did so without a word. "I do not know who is driving this car, but I can tell you that it is a 1990 pale blue Honda Civic with Virginia plates and the license number A678TZ. You need to be in our driveway in 30 seconds, or in 35 seconds, you will hear sirens and see blue lights flashing behind you. The choice is yours."

I hung up the phone. A mere 10 seconds later, the car sped back and ejected Persephone onto our lawn. It was comedic. She entered the house and I asked her to explain herself. Like a typical teenager, she stalled and refused to come clean about what was obviously happening.

Still calm, I took her cell phone and began to examine the log of the recent calls she had made and received. There were recent calls to and from 20 separate numbers.

"This is not quite enough people for a party, Persephone. Who else is coming?"

Trapped at last, she sighed, "That's it, Dad. Just those people. It wasn't a party. Just a get-together."

My daughter was sincere. She was so naïve that she didn't realize that five to six times the number of people she had just invited were planning to come to our house. Over the next 10 minutes, dozens of calls from people she did not know came to both our house phone and Persephone's cell, asking for directions. Slowly, she began to realize the magnitude of what she had almost gotten away with, and the damage that would have certainly been caused had her plans succeeded.

The Problem of Punishment

No sane person enjoys punishing his or her child. It is unpleasant for all concerned, and it takes a phenomenal amount of energy to enforce it. Add a whining teenager into the mix and it often seems easier just to yell until you feel better and then forget the whole thing ever happened. In my experience, this is what most parents do, and it is precisely why their children repeat negative behaviors over and over again.

I have always believed the punishment should fit the crime. It is no wiser to ground a child for a month for getting a B instead of an A, than it is to ignore a child who steals a hundred dollars out of your wallet. In Persephone's case, she had abused her freedom and my trust, so these are the things I immediately withheld. I took away her cell phone, also known as "oxygen" to a teenager, banned her use of the house phone, computer, TV, and grounded her from after-school activities other than those related to schoolwork. Naturally we spent that weekend in very close proximity to one another, even if it was rather quiet.

Once the dust from the initial event had settled, I asked her what she thought her punishment should be. I had urged her to use her weekend at home to consider the gravity of her actions, and I wanted to hear what she thought they warranted. To my shock, she told me that she thought she should be grounded for a year. She was so embarrassed by being outsmarted and caught in the act, and so struck by the fact that she had violated the trust of our relationship, that a yearlong grounding seemed reasonable to her as long as she could have access to her phone.

In the end, she was grounded for a matter of weeks, not months. She had no phone privileges and no rides or time with friends. She went to school, came home, and rode only with me. Unlike some of her friends, whose parents would ground them for a month and then look the other way when they went out two days later, Persephone's punishment lasted exactly as long as I said it would.

A Shocking Realization

Persephone was of course mortified by the entire affair. She returned to school on Monday, fully expecting to be ostracized by her friends and ridiculed for the incident. I felt bad for her, but I could not have cared less what her friends thought. Neither of us was prepared for what actually happened.

As expected, word of "The Party That Wasn't" had spread all over the school. Yet the reaction was quite the opposite of what Persephone, or I, could have predicted. Instead of ridicule, she was greeted with sympathy and hugs. As for me, I received some highly improbable attention. Instead of being viewed as an ogre, I was becoming a legendary figure: The Dad Who Outsmarted His Teenager.

What Persephone and I both learned from this unfortunate episode is that most of her friends were accustomed to deceiving and manipulating their parents with reckless abandon. The parents were too slow, too busy, or too snowed to notice the trivial changes in their children's behavior; worse yet, some were too disengaged to care. I became known among her peers as a father who was not only hard to trick, but who cared enough to find out what his daughter was up to. As Persephone grew older, her friends would flock to the house and often sought an opportunity to speak with me, or to solicit my opinion on matter of importance to them. This meant I got to play the role of CDO to a few of her friends as well.

Perhaps it is better to reflect on that day several months later, as opposed to soon after, when emotions are so high and feelings so complex that words could never explain! I was in love with you before I saw you, but that day I tasted the ultimate happiness, sense of accomplishment, pride, responsibility and joy! I looked at your little picture-perfect face, and I saw the world; your mother, myself, your grandparents everyone in you. It was the only time I felt immortal. Thank God for you!!

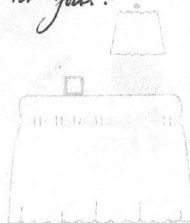

My entry on Persephone's Baby Diary. Early 1988.

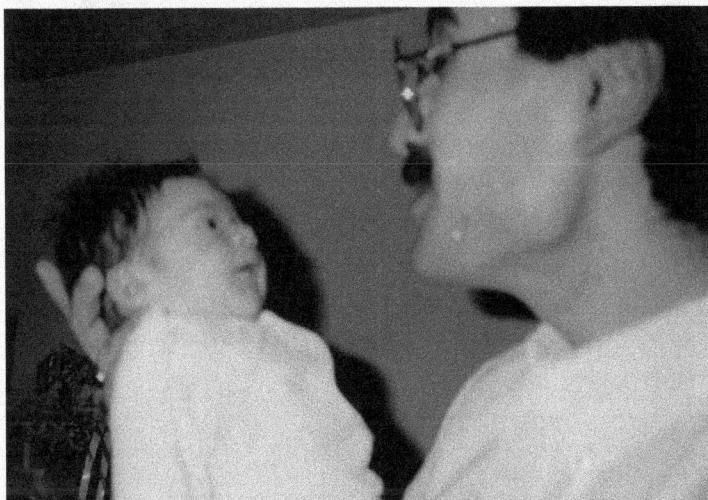

Looking into my newborn daughter's eyes. November, 1987.

Persephone with my parents. June, 1988.

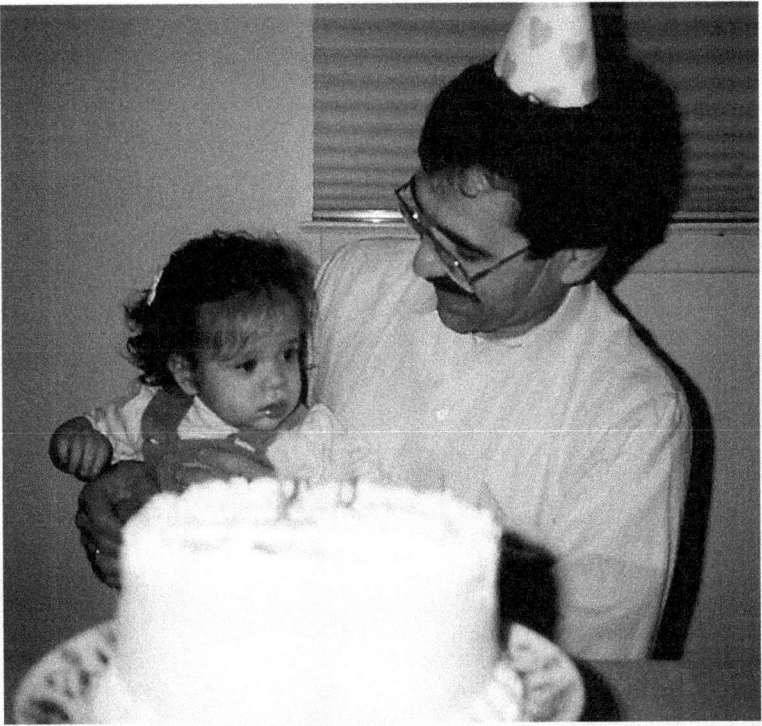

Persephone's 1st Birthday. November, 1988.

I always loved her hugs! March, 1989.

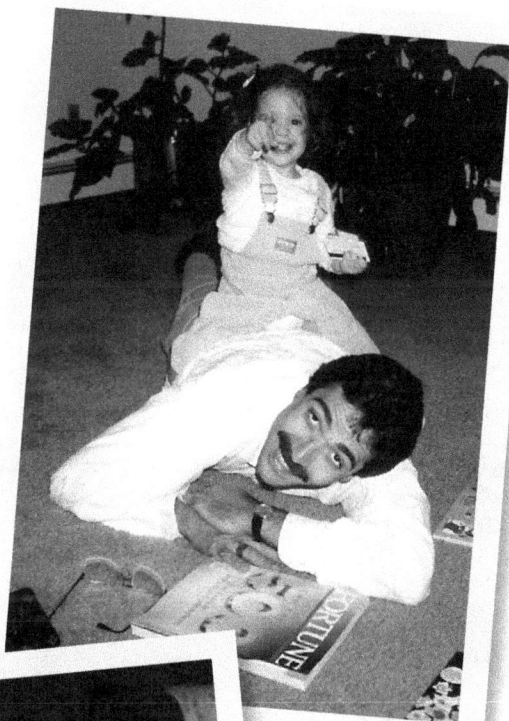

Executive by day,
jungle gym by night.
May, 1989.

Walking in my shoes!
October, 1989.

A kiss for Santa Christmas 1989.

Learning to read.
Madeline was her
favorite book.
March, 1990.

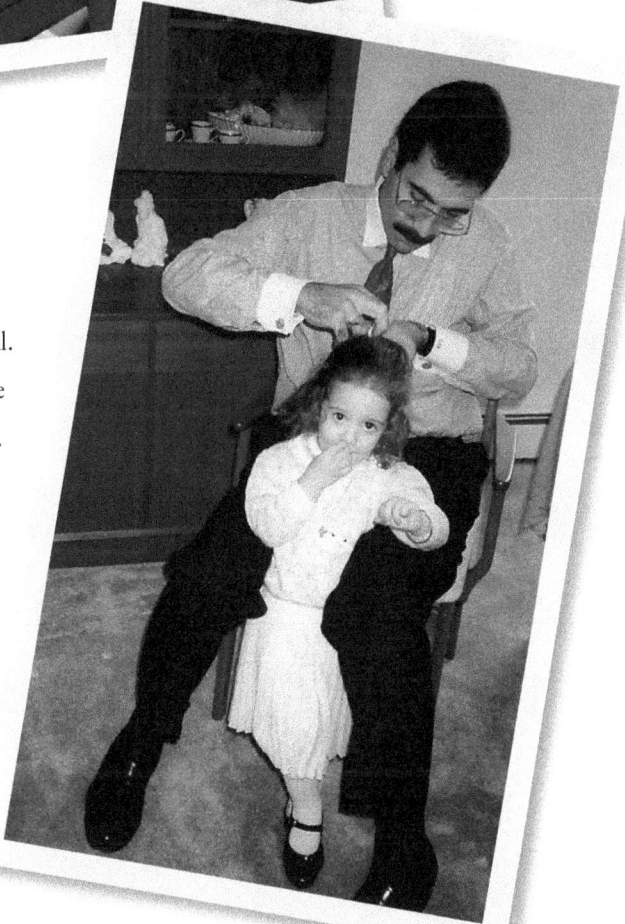

Sunday morning ritual.
Fixing her hair before
church. April, 1990.

On vacation in Greece. Summer 1993.

Our first father-daughter portrait. June, 1994.

Part II

The

CDO OPERATING MANUAL

"If we do not both see and hear our children, how will we know what they are thinking? And if we do not know what they are thinking, how can we influence their thinking to maximize the good and avoid disasters?"

CHAPTER 5

———— ❦ ————

EFFECTIVE
COMMUNICATION

WE HAVE ALL HEARD THAT CHILDREN ARE to be seen and not heard. This might work well enough for a formal dinner party but does not work at all for life. For those who actually believe this, my advice to you is buckle up, because it's going to be a bumpy ride.

If we do not both see and hear our children, how will we know what they are thinking? And if we do not know what they are thinking, how can we influence their thinking to maximize the good and avoid disasters? Communicating with our children, whether they are 16 months or 16 years old, can be one of the most challenging aspects of parenting. While it is one of the most important parts of being a parent, it is also one of the most rewarding. It is here where we can apply a lot of what works in the office.

Control Your Emotions

We have already discussed the importance of self-awareness at home and at work. Our credibility is dependent on our ability not to overreact or under react to the situations we encounter. Put another way, our credibility depends on being cool-headed. Had I caustically vented my anger and disappointment at Persephone for her secret party attempt, I would have damaged our mutual respect and trust and driven her further away. On the other hand, had I let the whole thing go, my house might have been destroyed, and I would have set Persephone up for even more outrageous behavior in the future.

> ## *"Parenting requires deliberate, rational responses, except that nothing about raising a child is cold or unemotional."*

With this example in mind, let's examine how to control our emotions while communicating. Let's consider the business world first. This is in many ways simpler, because most of our interactions at work are not as emotionally loaded as they can be at home. The desirable outcome is almost always clear, even when emotions are involved. For instance, if you were a company executive with a lot riding on securing a big contract, nobody would expect you to be happy if you were not awarded that business. In fact, it would seem flippant and irresponsible to brush it off as unimportant.

Additionally, a mature executive cannot become distressed or overly anxious without compromising his ability to lead. A measured, reasonable response might be to say something like, "OK, we've been dealt this blow and I know it hurts, but we're going to face it, evaluate why it happened, learn from it, and things will be all right." This acknowledges the reality of the situation, encourages productive next steps, and shows your humanity. It demonstrates that as the leader you feel the same pain they do but refuse to be paralyzed by it. You pull yourself together and march on.

Parenting requires the same kind of deliberate, rational responses, except that nothing about raising a child is cold or unemotional. It is very tempting to overreact when children do things that irritate us or strike at particular places in our hearts. However, maintaining your composure is even more important with your children than it is with your employees. Just like at work, you need to keep your end goals in mind: What do you want to come out of this interaction? Too many parents speak with the goal of relieving the anger they feel. While this is a completely normal desire, you must resist the urge to lash out. You must keep your cool.

Only when you maintain an appropriate and measured response will communication get you closer to your goals. Children look to your reactions to gauge their own. If you begin an interaction with anger and frustration evident in your voice, one of two things will happen: Your child will escalate the emotion by responding the same way, or he will shut down entirely, isolating himself from you. Neither of these outcomes moves you closer to raising a responsible, self-sufficient adult.

At work there are times I must remind myself that I am the leader. Other people may be acting less than levelheaded, but I cannot join that parade. At home I had to remind myself that I was the parent: I was the adult, not the child. When I discovered Persephone's party plans I had to be careful not to let my anger and disappointment poison my communication to her. I had to base the words and tone of voice I chose on the facts of the situation and my goals for her, not on my feelings. By keeping my voice and words even and measured but not unemotional or detached, I showed her respect, retained her respect, and achieved my desired conclusion: She never tried a stunt like that again.

"When you can recognize your own mistakes, quirks or even weaknesses, and can laugh at them, you become approachable to everyone around you."

Caution: Laughter Attracts People

Comedian Ron White gives this advice: "I believe when life gives you lemons, you should make lemonade...and try to find someone whose life has given them vodka, and have a party."

Conflict is inevitable for every boss and every parent. Though we must always keep our emotions in check, we must also try not to take things too seriously. Bear in mind that occasional disagreement is not the end of the world: in fact, it is healthy and normal. And sometimes, the most appropriate reaction is to laugh.

One summer afternoon when Persephone was in high school, I saw her and her boyfriend (who was not my favorite person) innocently lying in the hammock. From a few yards away, I exclaimed at the top of my lungs "No two persons will ever be horizontal at any time under this roof." As soon as this brilliant statement left my mouth, I continued in the same loud voice "This is the dumbest thing I've ever heard myself say!" and we all laughed out loud. Since then, every time I saw Persephone lying on the couch alone watching TV she would mimic my voice, repeating my earlier admonition, and we'd both laugh.

Of course, we must be careful to laugh with our children, not at them. We do not want to hurt their feelings, and every parent knows the unbelievable fragility of children's emotions. The good news is that as a parent or a boss it is always OK to laugh at yourself. When you can recognize your own mistakes, quirks or even weaknesses, and can laugh at them, you become approachable to everyone around you. The more approachable you are, the better your communications will be both at work and at home.

"It is OK not to be liked sometimes. Not being respected is never acceptable, and trading respect for popularity is always a losing proposition."

There is another extreme to being unapproachable, and that is prematurely trying to be your child's friend. Too many parents are so concerned with their children liking them that they shy away from giving clear instructions or enforcing rules. Think about how this plays out in a typical office environment. A boss who is so eager for all his employees to like him will rob himself of his ability to lead and will soon lose their respect. Before long, all the workers are doing whatever they want and chaos ensues. It is OK not to be liked sometimes. Not being respected is never acceptable, and trading respect for popularity is always a losing proposition.

The same goes with our kids. Every child is born wanting to please his parents. You do not have to win your child's approval, but you can never risk losing his respect. Even a grumpy teenager wants your love whether she admits it or not. So stick to the rules, keep a good sense of humor, and don't forget to tell them that you love them.

"Above everything else, listening and observing your children shows them you respect them."

Remember to Listen and Be Emotionally Available

When we go to the movies we see the product of a long process. First there was the concept, screenplay and the casting, then the filming and the editing. What we may not realize is that this long process involves feedback at every single stage. Screenplays are rewritten several times; actors cast may or may not work out, and over the course of editing entire scenes can be deleted from the original film.

"We need to listen to our kids as much as possible, and think about what they are saying. Only when we spend time listening can we adjust our parenting so that the end product (the adult we raise) is everything he or she can be."

Producers want to bring the most marketable product to a theater near you. To do this, they solicit opinions – both from experts and focus groups – throughout the very expensive process of making a movie. They adjust what they do based on what they hear. As parents, we need to do the same thing. We need to listen to our kids as much as possible, and think about what they are saying. Only when we spend time listening can we adjust our parenting so that the end product (the adult we raise) is everything he or she can be.

Every child is different. If you have a talkative child, your challenge will be making time to listen and not tune him out. Stay engaged with him, he'll do the same with you. If your child is quiet, you must learn to ask the right questions to get the ball rolling. Younger children often say exactly what is on their minds, whereas teenagers may talk around a subject, particularly if something is bothering them.

Try asking open-ended questions that cannot be answered with a yes or no. Instead of asking, "How was your day today?" to which the predictable answer is "Fine," try saying, "Tell me what happened at school today." You might be surprised at the reply. Like any other skill, reading your child's moods and concerns takes time. Each minute you log listening gets you closer to mastery!

Every so often, ask yourself how well you know your child and give yourself a pop quiz. Go ahead, take the quiz now, you'll be the only one to see your grade.

As a parent, you should readily know the answers to these questions and recognize that the answers will change rapidly as time goes by. My mother did this masterfully. In contrast to my father, she knew details about our friends, our interests, our likes and dislikes, our fears and aspirations, and over time she became the parent we felt most comfortable talking to.

Life moves quickly, and it is easy for us to forget how quickly our children grow. I once knew a man who gave his 22-year-old daughter a pink kitchen appliance because he knew pink to be her favorite color. Although she joyfully accepted the present, she confessed later that pink had not been her favorite color since she was 6!

Parental Unit Pop Quiz

1. What are your child's likes?

    a. _____

    b. _____

    c. _____

2. What are her dislikes?

    a. _____

    b. _____

    c. _____

3. Who are her best friends?

    a. _____

    b. _____

    c. _____

    d. _____

    e. _____

4. How is school or work going? (Give a one- to two-sentence answer)

5. What are her interests or hobbies?

    a. _____

    b. _____

    c. _____

6. What is her favorite music? (You may list genres, songs or artists)

    a. _____

    b. _____

    c. _____

"Every so often, ask yourself how well you know your child and give yourself a pop quiz."

Remember in your listening also to observe actions both obvious and subtle. Perhaps your 10-year-old says school is going well, but she becomes anxious before she leaves each morning. Maybe your son insists he loves basketball just like you, but does not seem excited for practice or games. Paying attention to these kinds of behaviors can give you valuable insight into your child's needs and can help to inform your decisions.

"Remember in your listening also to observe actions both obvious and subtle."

Take the time to examine the things your children draw, write or produce. I had the habit of collecting all the things Persephone made in school or at home, whether it was artwork or even handwritten notes. I was interested in anything my child made. Still, I couldn't have imagined the impression that my collection of these little artifacts would make on Persephone. Yet she wrote to me at age 9:

"Take the time to examine the things your children draw, write or produce."

December 29,96

Dear Daddy,

Sorry?! Sorry !!! I bet you are saying to yourself, "Why is she saying sorry?" I was looking for a shirt in your closet so I could go to bed. Well then I saw a ticket. No maybe two tickets. Yes two tickets. Well anyways I was I looked in it I saw the things from Fathers Day. (at Norwood). I also saw pictures of me. But what I'm really trying too say is thank you, thank you for Collecting my stuff. And again sorry!

Above everything else, listening and observing your children shows them you respect them. Always bear in mind, our goal is to raise a dependable, conscientious, reliable, trustworthy, sensible, self-sufficient, un-entitled, mature adult; an adult who respects herself and treats others with respect. Showing our children the respect of earnest listening, advances this goal like nothing else.

Can you still communicate effectively if you are not home every night? If, like me, you are among the parents who travel for business, you may think that you are at a disadvantage because of the physical space periodically separating you from your child. While this may be true in some cases, you can narrow or even bridge physical distance with emotional availability. Conversely, no amount of physical closeness can compensate for the void left by a lack of emotional availability.

While editing this chapter, Persephone wrote: "You were always available, even when you were overseas. You valued and cherished the moments we had together. Remembering details matters; being able to spit those details back years later means that you valued our time."

Two-Way Traffic

Whether in the office or in the living room, effective communication is a dialogue, not a monologue. Unfortunately, when more than one person is involved in a conversation, there is the potential for misunderstanding. Confusion and miscommunication can range from humorous to disastrous. The best way to guard against this is to think deliberately about how we communicate, being mindful of our tone of voice, our choice of words, our body language. We must also think about our audience and prepare accordingly.

Why is it that some of us will spend hours perfecting a sales pitch, but spend little thought on how we interact with our children? Certainly, our livelihood may depend on that sale, but much of our home's harmony depends on our ability to communicate effectively with our kids. This does not mean that family life is not full of spontaneous exchanges that we do not think about at all, just like our interactions at work. It just means that our communication will only get better if we take time to examine it critically from time to time.

Consider this proven sales technique. You have delivered your sales pitch flawlessly and it is time to close and ask for a commitment. To do this, pose an open-ended question such as, "Based on everything we have discussed, do you see any reason why this product is not the perfect fit for your needs?" And then be quiet. The first person to speak following the question will almost always be the one who agrees to your request. The technique takes discipline to learn, but it is really quite easy. Ask your question, and then resist the urge to fill the quiet until the other person responds. If you can master that, you will find that you've usually elicited the desired response. Most of the time, the speaker will not want to disappoint. The person will either answer affirmatively or will give you information you can use to your advantage.

Parents, on the other hand, tend to be masters of the monologue: the irritating speech that puts everyone in the audience to sleep. This is true whether you are lecturing your 6-year-old on picking up his toys or your teenager on getting his grades under control. A monologue pushes information on the listener; it does not welcome information back. Not only is there no way for the listener to respond, there is no way for the talker to know if he's being understood.

As a parent, do not let yourself get caught in the monologue trap. Instead, learn to ask those open-ended questions. "Honey, how are your toys supposed to look?" "Son, what needs to happen to get these grades to an acceptable level?" Then wait. Refrain from saying all the things you want to say: ("You know that your dolls shouldn't be all over the floor! No college will accept you with C's in math!") Let your child talk to you, and be silent. You'll be surprised how much of what you wanted to say to him actually comes out of his mouth. The biggest advantage of all this is that because he feels he received the courtesy and respect he deserves, he will repay you with the same. This is indeed the win-win scenario.

Communication is a two-way street—a street that should have a lot of traffic moving in both directions. Life gets busy, but make sure you are making time to communicate with your kids on a daily basis. A lapse in communication is almost always interpreted negatively. Children will feel you don't care, you are mad, or you're too wrapped up in your work. Even the most sullen teenager secretly wants to know that you care. Consistent communication is one of the best ways to guard against miscommunication.

It Is OK to Disagree

Whether you run a company or a department of one, you know it is impossible to have uniform opinions about everything. So why would we expect our kids to think exactly like we do? Sometimes the most heartfelt discussions with your kids reach an impasse. I have at times failed to convince my daughter of something and she has failed to convince me. I don't mean that we refused to give in to the other out of stubbornness; we legitimately did not see eye to eye. And we learned together that this was OK. It was more important to me to raise a daughter who could think for herself than to agree all the time.

What is not OK during a disagreement is to storm out of the room. Persephone tried this a few times when she was younger. We would reach that impasse in our discussion and she would get up and walk away. I was irritated with her behavior to no end, but instead of yelling, I explained to her in a stern but polite way exactly how I felt: "I expect you to treat my opinion with the same level of respect as you want me to treat yours. If you storm out when I express a viewpoint you don't like, don't expect me to even entertain a discussion of the next thing that is important to you. You will likely be pleading your case to my empty chair."

Instead of venting my frustration at her, I taught her that I expected her to invest in our relationship in exactly the same way I did. I explained that because I always treated her with the respect I believed she deserved, I expected the same treatment in return and that the reciprocity was not optional.

As a boss or manager, you can talk about the things that irritate you with colleagues at your level or above you. If your practice is to unload your frustrations on your subordinates, you automatically lose their respect and your ability to lead them. Of course all of us have let a self-contradictory order slip out with our kids: "Didn't you hear what I just said to you?" we'll ask, or seem to invite further details by asking "Please explain to me how could this have happened?"

Then, when the child tries to respond or explain, we add: "Don't talk back to me!" or "I am not interested in hearing anything that comes out of your mouth." These silly exchanges are bound to happen now and then, but do your best to keep them to a minimum and apologize when you've calmed down.

Although storming out is never OK, sometimes it is best to halt the discussion if one or both of you are getting too emotional. We must remember that children are children: They get moody and struggle with controlling their tempers or their tears. Sometimes more talking will only fuel the fire; if you give the subject a rest, cooler heads will prevail.

When you choose to shelve the discussion, be deliberate with your words and set a specific point in time when you'll both come back to the table and revisit the issue. Otherwise you will be perceived as the parent who uses a time-out to stop a discussion in hopes that your child will either forget or tire of it. In my experience, each time I suggested revisiting an unresolved issue at a later time, Persephone's first question was, "When?" When we reopened the discussion, I was always surprised and impressed that she came back with well-thought-out arguments that, more often than not, convinced me in whole or at least in part.

"Parents tend to be masters of the monologue: the irritating speech that puts everyone in the audience to sleep."

Here is a tip I learned at the office that will score you big points at home. If you are the highest-ranking person in an organization or in a division, all good and bad things stop at your doorstep. There is honor in accepting responsibility for a mistake or wrongdoing. When you do, you will surprise your employees for doing the unthinkable, and earn their respect. I have been fortunate to experience that on several occasions.

As a parent, you are the highest-ranking person in your family. If you dare apologize to your children for a mistake or misunderstanding, you will witness the most impressive transformation of your relationship. You will blow their minds. You'll have shown them that you are human, just like them. That like them, you are not infallible and that being accountable for your mistakes is honorable. You will discover that they will soon follow your example.

"If you dare apologize to your children for a mistake or misunderstanding, you will witness the most impressive transformation of your relationship. You will blow their minds."

Respect and Foster Independent Thought

Wise women have observed that the qualities that make for a "good" boyfriend are not necessarily those that make a good husband. The wild, unpredictable heartthrob in a romantic comedy may be great for a few dates, but he'll probably be an unreliable partner in life. In the same way, the quiet, compliant child who never does or says anything to displease you may be an easy 6-year-old, but she may not make a very strong adult.

Allowing your children to speak their minds in a respectful manner encourages them to develop the thinking skills they will need for the rest of their lives. Don't shut them down like a tyrant, but don't let them become dictators.

Remember that power cannot persuade the heart. A boss that rules with an iron fist will lose every employee who can find a better opportunity, leaving him with the "rubber stamps." The parent who runs a house that way will either lose his child when she's old enough to leave or will raise an adult utterly dependent on a stronger person to tell him what to do. You don't have an obligation to give them the answer they think they want, but you do have a responsibility to listen and help guide their thinking.

In business, the most valuable people are those who can solve problems creatively by introducing fresh ideas and solutions. Those who never ask "why" may be too willing to comply with the status quo and are less likely to proffer new solutions. Others are simply not invested enough in the company to care. Understand that it is not your authority that persuades. It is your reasoning and your care.

Only weak leaders view questions as an attack on their authority, and it is their loss as well as their employees'. Stifling creativity and discouraging alternative perspectives on problems leads to the kind of myopic decision-making that drives entire industries out of business. Embracing the ingenuity of your employees brings out their best and the best for your company.

The same is true at home. Two-way communication with our kids not only strengthens our relationships with them, it also nurtures their imagination and confidence. If we think their viewpoints are important, they will too. By discouraging questions and squelching independent thought, we are telling them that they do not have anything valuable to contribute.

Expect pushback and welcome it. You are not wasting your time by doing so; you are investing in your child. As we were reviewing this chapter, Persephone commented: "You put me in my place after letting me push back at you. I have always respected you for that." Seize pushback as an opportunity to converse with and motivate your child.

I always tried to create an environment where my daughter and her friends could ask unusual questions, and I would try to give thoughtful answers. I was shocked at how many of her friends—friends with loving, supportive parents—responded to this like someone getting a drink of water after a day in the desert. These children craved the opportunity to ask serious questions of adults, such as "How do I navigate through life's challenges?" "How can I honestly talk with my parents without being judged?" and my personal favorite "How did you and Persephone develop this kind of relationship?"

"Understand that it is not your authority that persuades. It is your reasoning and your care."

If all this communication sounds like a lot of work, it is. However, the reward is greater than you can imagine. One day you will look at your child and see a mature, confident adult who is taking care of himself and making a contribution to society. You will also have a strong relationship built on years of talking and listening. I would not trade that for anything.

"Empowering your children means giving them the wisdom and skills they need to make good decisions for their current stage of life."

CHAPTER 6

─────────── ❦ ───────────

EMPOWERING
YOUR CHILD

BILL GATES SAID OF THE INFORMATION TECHNOLOGY REVOLU-TION, "There's a basic philosophy here that by empowering...workers you'll make their jobs far more interesting, and they'll be able to work at a higher level than they would have without all that information just a few clicks away." We can readily see how this philosophy is applied in the business world. Empowered employees are more invested in their jobs and bring their best to what they do. Good managers under-stand that imaginative problem-solving is far preferable to mindless compliance.

The principle can be a little trickier to apply to parenting. What does it really mean to empower your child so that he or she is deeply invested in your family? You are not going to hand the car keys over to your 10-year-old, nor are you going to hand your teenager a wad of cash and tell her to spend it on whatever she likes. Empowering your children means giving them the wisdom and skills they need to make good decisions for their current stage of life. If you do this for long enough, they will be ready to make decisions as an adult. In fact, the process of parenting can be seen as the transition from taking care of your child to empowering him to take care of himself.

The Whys

Remember all those "why" questions we talked about earlier? I found that answering Persephone's endless "whys" was vital to empowering her to become her own person. When we do not take the time to thoughtfully answer our children's questions, we can be unintentionally dismissive. We are sending the silent message that they do not need to know more than they already do, or that they are not important enough for us to bother explaining something.

"Giving your children a sound explanation for why you do what you do gives them a reason to follow the rules even outside of your presence. It also forces you to think more deliberately about the rules you set."

Of course these "whys" begin very early—usually at the ripe old age of 2 or 3. Certainly there will be times when children use the "why" as a stall: "Why do I have to go to bed now, Daddy?" The key is to give younger children a true but succinct answer and move on. As the child grows, however, you will need to set aside real time to answer his questions thoughtfully.

Often your children will question why you are making a certain decision or the reasoning behind a certain rule. It is easy to feel as if this is a challenge to your authority. However, keep in mind that it is far easier to accept a ruling if you understand the reasoning behind it. As we discussed previously, giving your children a sound explanation for why you do what you do gives them a reason to follow the rules even outside of your presence. It also forces you to think more deliberately about the rules you set.

Be prepared for your children to ask you "why" about other things too. Once again, remember that all children are different and therefore curious about different things. Do not allow yourself to see this as a nuisance. This is your opportunity to share your knowledge and experiences with them. If you don't know the answer, offer to help them look it up. If your children see you as a reliable source of information from a young age, they will continue to seek your advice as they get older. From her late teens to the present, Persephone has consulted me on personal and business matters far more frequently than I could have ever imagined, which has been an honor and joy.

The Hows

Consider the expertise and confidence required to perform a routine surgical procedure, such as a tonsillectomy. First a doctor must complete her undergraduate education, four years of medical school, and then an intense internship, watching and learning from other doctors. After that, during her residency, she will need to observe and assist with procedures many times before finally performing them herself under close supervision. Slowly but surely she will gain the experience and confidence to not only perform the procedure unsupervised, but also teach others to do so.

The good news about parenting is that you don't have to train your children to be surgeons, engineers or plumbers. You just have to train them to be adults, and you already know how to do that. Remember that parenthood is mentorship. A mentor does not micromanage the process by which you get from point A to point B. Nor does he stand back and watch you as you try to figure the process by yourself. Instead, he works shoulder to shoulder with you throughout the process. Sometimes the mentor works ahead, showing you how it is to be done. Other times he is working just behind you, affirming your progress and standing by to catch anything that may go wrong.

Effective mentorship requires confidence and humility. Yet so many parents today are hesitant to advise their children on what is right and wrong and how to make wise decisions. Can you imagine if the young surgical resident was instructed by a doctor who said things like, "Well, I don't want tell you how to do this. What do you think is best?" On the other hand, a confident mentor is also humble enough to admit that he makes mistakes too. I did my best to make sure that I let Persephone learn from my mistakes as well as my successes.

"From her late teens to the present, Persephone has consulted me on personal and business matters far more frequently than I could have ever imagined, which has been an honor and joy."

Some Lessons From Socrates

Although Socrates and I both hail from Greece, I never had the pleasure of being directly instructed by him for obvious reasons. His methods of instruction, however, have much to offer us today. He demonstrated a way by which teachers could instruct and empower their students at the same time.

> *"When we employ the Socratic Method of teaching in parenting, we are showing our kids that we believe our point of view can stand on its merits, not just our authority."*

The Socratic method of teaching requires debate. It forces both student and teacher to back up their hypotheses with supporting evidence, and trains the mind to search for inconsistencies. It demands much more in-depth thinking than the "instruction and regurgitation" method popular in schools today. It does not require that the teacher and student disagree: indeed the teacher will often take the opposing position in a debate to help the student develop a more firm sense of her point of view.

When we employ this method in parenting, we are showing our kids that we believe our point of view can stand on its merits, not just our authority. This becomes increasingly important as our children grow older. In the spring of Persephone's junior year of high school, she had a boyfriend whom I'll call Troy. Troy was not a bad kid, but he was not particularly motivated. He was a couple of years older than Persephone, and was taking a few classes at the local community college while working. By my evaluation, his choices in life had been consistently less than ideal.

Needless to say, I was not thrilled with the relationship. Persephone was not quite an adult; however, I knew that insisting that she end the relationship would do no good. I also knew she was not anxious to leave him to go away to college and that their attachment to each other might become a real obstacle to Persephone's future success. I pondered all this on a daily basis while saying very little.

One morning, after all her college applications had been submitted, Persephone approached me tentatively. "Dad," she said, "I think I want to take a year off before going to college."

"Why?" I asked.

"Well, I'm just really stressed out with my work at school. I feel like I need a break from being a full-time student." I knew she just didn't want to leave Troy behind, but I did not say this.

"Persephone," I answered, "I think that's a marvelous idea. This is probably the only time in your life when you can take a year off without worrying about it." I said nothing more, observing that she was surprised by my response.

"OK," she continued. "I was thinking that I would take a few classes at community college and work part-time in retail."

"I see," I replied. "But, that's not really an option for a year off. This is a wonderful opportunity for expanding your horizons by serving others. I propose you decide between joining the Peace Corps or AmeriCorps." Persephone was stunned. She looked at me as if I had grown a second head! I explained to her what each organization did, how any of the colleges to which she got accepted would happily defer her admission for a year, and offered to help her apply to either program.

When she protested, we entered a brief discussion of the merits of her plan versus mine. She could not say that I was being inflexible, because I fully supported her idea of taking a year off. She was forced to defend her plan against a better one, instead of preserving her right to forgo college for a year. In the end, she went off to her four-year institution quite happily, leaving Troy behind.

Now, I am fairly certain if I had just ordered Persephone off to college without listening to her reasons for wanting a break, she would have found a way to rebel. Certainly, she might have complied with my wishes, but her heart would have been eager to be rid of my authority and influence at the first opportunity. On the other hand, if I had allowed her to waste a year of her life with a boy going nowhere, I would have set her up for innumerable further mistakes.

The Socratic method of debate and instruction helps build a long-lasting relationship with your child. It teaches them to support their beliefs with evidence, as well as thoughtfully consider the evidence presented by others. We need to remember that our kids will not always *have* to listen to us: active debates and discussions can help them *want* to listen to us. Often these kinds of discussions, as long as we remember to be mature and controlled, will help us find common ground even in a seemingly insurmountable disagreement.

The fact is that most teenagers know when they are being ridiculous. They often want to test the waters to see if we will call them out. I'm happy to say that Persephone and I have laughed many times about her "year off" proposal, now that it is far behind us.

"We need to remember that our kids will not always have to listen to us: active debates and discussions can help them want to listen to us."

Avoid the Buddy System:
You Are NOT Your Child's Buddy

While mentioned earlier, let us now address what I believe to be a prevailing myth in parenting today: that to truly empower your child you must prematurely become his or her "buddy" or friend. I say prematurely because I believe that our children can become our dear friends when they are fully grown adults. Indeed, this is one of the greatest rewards of successful parenthood. But in the meantime you do not need to be your child's buddy to empower him. In fact, you may unwittingly do just the opposite.

"You do not need to be your child's buddy to empower him. In fact, you may unwittingly do just the opposite."

The Buddy System of parenting did not exist in the culture in which I grew up. I got to know it as I watched the parents of some of Persephone's friends, and frankly, I found it disturbing. The essence of parental mentorship is modeling and teaching how to be a responsible adult. If you become your child's buddy too soon, you will in effect lower yourself to her level. You will not be modeling adulthood, but instead will be acting like a child yourself. How is this possibly helpful?

As the parent, you must be their trusted, honest—often constructively critical but never judgmental—mentor to whom they can feel comfortable to turn with any issue. You will not hold their hands every step of the way. You will not simply tell them what to do or how to do it, but you will give them the tools and the guidance of your experience and insights that will enable them to choose the right course of action for themselves.

"The essence of parental mentorship is modeling and teaching how to be a responsible adult."

Remember that kids naturally think they know more than they do. Empowering them means giving them opportunities to gain knowledge and experience so they will actually know what they are doing, not pretending they are as clever as they think. You wouldn't hand a teenager the car keys if he had no driving experience and call that empowerment. You would make sure he passed his driver's education class and take him for behind-the-wheel hours. The same instruction and mentorship goes into every part of life.

We empower children to make decisions not by pretending they already know everything they need to know, but by helping them think through decisions sensibly. I had a wonderful teaching opportunity with Persephone when she was in college deciding where to go abroad for a semester. I had already planted the idea in her mind that she would need to spend some time overseas. Based on my own experience as a young person, I knew this to be a tremendously valuable part of growing up.

Like any normal young woman, Persephone thought first of fun and second of the long-term value of the experience. She informed me that she'd found an exchange student program that she wanted to do with a friend. "The program includes two weeks in residence at a university in Australia," she told me, "and after that my friend and I will travel for a couple of weeks all over Asia."

"That'd be a wonderful plan," I replied. "But as you clearly know, I am happy to finance your education, not your vacation." And with this admonition, I asked her to revise her plans and find a more suitable program that offered more valuable exposure so we could discuss its merits.

> *"We empower children to make decisions not by pretending they already know everything they need to know, but by helping them think through decisions sensibly."*

Persephone ended up spending three months in London working for a global nonprofit organization in exchange for college credits. She was not only featured in a 2009 fall issue of *Vogue* in France for the projects with which she was involved, but she discovered firsthand how fulfilling it was to do meaningful work. She was able to interact with very influential people on a daily basis, as well as navigate a world-class city on her own. She came home far more mature, confident and experienced, and with some great new items on her resume. She also took advantage of her three-day weekends to visit four other European countries. Mission accomplished!

Again, I could have yelled at her for being foolish and wanting to tan with her friends instead of learning and experiencing new things, but that would have only encouraged rebellion. On the other hand, I could have been her buddy and allowed her to do as she pleased, which would have resulted in a wasted summer. By examining my information and perspective, she was able to have an even more empowering experience, and come back even better prepared for adulthood.

There was nothing wrong with Persephone's desire to essentially spend a semester on vacation; it just wasn't the best choice for her future. I helped her understand this not by being her friend but by being her parent. I empowered her and guided her to make the right decision.

When the Choice Is Theirs

From the moment Persephone was born, I knew the day would come when she would have a choice of whether to listen to me or not. I didn't know it would come when she was just 10 years old. After two years of separation, custody battles and general unpleasantness, my divorce from Persephone's mother was final. I had taken my daughter on vacation, providing one of those much-needed opportunities to give her my undivided attention for a while. The morning of our second day away, the phone rang.

It was her mother, explaining that she was moving to a different city and taking Persephone with her. My heart dropped. In all my planning and calculation as a father, I had never dreamed my ex-wife would try to take our child from me. I wondered how much of this plan Persephone already knew. After collecting my thoughts and purging the flood of emotions, at least temporarily, I asked Persephone to join me for a walk on the beach, where I explained the news to her.

"That's funny," she responded. "She never told me anything about that. She can move wherever she wants to; I'm staying here with you."

I smiled. Deep inside, I felt extremely gratified. She was a little girl, of course, so I knew she might change her mind. Thankfully she did not, and I was blessed from that point forward to immerse myself in being her father. Now both of us look back on that decision as the best thing that ever happened to either of us.

CHAPTER 7

MANAGING THE UPS AND DOWNS

PHILOSOPHER GEORGE SANTAYANA OBSERVED THAT, "The young man who has not wept is a savage, and the old man who will not laugh is a fool." Deeply felt emotions enrich our lives, and yet they can also be hugely destructive. We all understand that a healthy childhood will have its share of laughter and tears, but how can we prevent powerful feelings from taking over our lives?

As we journey through life, we want to experience and understand our emotions, but we do not want our emotions to direct the journey. Different cultures and generations have approached this problem in various ways. Some suppress emotions to the point of denying their existence, while others indulge them with shouting matches and hysterics. To strike a healthy balance, we must learn to manage our emotions effectively and express them appropriately, while teaching our children to do the same.

"As we journey through life, we want to experience and understand our emotions, but we do not want our emotions to direct the journey."

Being Cool Is Hot, But Being Hot Is Not Cool

Most sensible people stop worrying about acting cool sometime in their mid-20s; however, countless parents have tried to stay cool in an often-pointless effort to keep up with their children and win their approval. The one way we can all be "cool" parents is to keep calm when our children are at their most challenging.

Learning to do this requires a hefty dose of pragmatism. We are all human. Life in general and children in particular can be very frustrating. As I mentioned earlier, this is where a healthy dose of self-awareness comes into play. Pay attention to what bothers you most in your interactions with your children and ask yourself why it bothers you. People have different personalities. Maybe you need quiet to concentrate and your child loves talking constantly throughout the day. These kinds of differences require sensible compromise, such as some agreed-upon quiet time for Mommy or Daddy and some set-aside listening time for daughter.

"Out-of-control, hot-headed emotions can lead to a "process failure" in your parenting and damage your relationship with your child."

On the other hand, our emotional reactions sometimes are rooted in past experiences. Fear, above all other emotions, causes irrational behavior. What do you fear the most? That others won't respect or love you? That you will fail to measure up? Maybe you fear illness or catastrophe or other phenomena over which you have little or no control.

One of my greatest fears has always been disappointing people. From my parents and siblings, to my daughter and my employees, I have always been conscious of those who depend on me to do the right thing. I suppose what it comes down to is the fact that my biggest fear has been disappointing myself.

As Persephone was growing up she would, of course, express her discontent at various times; I had to be careful not to take this personally. I had to distinguish between failing to provide her with what she needed versus giving her what she wanted. As her father, it was my job to see the difference. I also found that as I reacted to Persephone with calm, it encouraged her to calm down as well. Of course this works both ways: out of control emotions on your part will encourage your child to respond in kind.

In business we learn as much from our failures as from our successes. Failure analysis is not self-berating, but a vital part of growth. W. Edwards Deming, originator of TQM (total quality management), said that 95 percent of failures are process failures, as opposed to defects in a component or design. Neither you nor your child is defective, but out-of-control, hot-headed emotions can lead to a "process failure" in your parenting and damage your relationship with your child.

Live Your Own Life and Let Your Children Live Theirs

We have talked quite a bit about highly motivated parents who often unintentionally neglect their children. But there is another common "process failure" among parents who, while devoted to their children, try to live vicariously through them. These types of parents want their children to play a sport, go to a particular school, or enter a specific field because of their own unfulfilled dreams. Other parents simply take their child's successes and failures personally, reacting as if they, themselves, were experiencing them.

Parents of this sort are often willing to sacrifice anything just to give their child some sort of advantage. In this way, they appear to be quite selfless. Consider the following parents: Susan was a talented athlete growing up, but wasn't quite good enough to realize her dreams of running in the Olympics. When her daughter showed some promise in gymnastics, she began to pay hundreds of extra dollars a month to get her private lessons in addition to her regular training.

"I always tried to remember that I was mentoring Persephone to live the life that she would choose for herself. I wanted her to be a happy and productive adult, but she did not have to follow in my footsteps or fulfill my own lost childhood dreams."

John was always socially awkward as a child and longed to be popular. He spends thousands of dollars each year throwing elaborate parties for his son to try to win him friends. To a casual observer, nothing is wrong. What could possibly be the problem with getting your daughter a private gymnastics lesson or throwing your son a party you can afford? The issue is the underlying motivation: Susan's bitterness over her unfulfilled dreams and John's insecurity over his childhood experiences.

These negative parental emotions, if not dealt with properly, will put too much pressure on children. Since the parents are using their children to try to become happy, the children will feel responsible for the parents' emotional state. In these cases, Susan's daughter had to quit her sport after suffering overuse injuries, and John's son became sullen and withdrawn for most of his teenage years.

In many instances, this issue can be further magnified with predictably deleterious effects to the children. One such instance is when parents divorce and their children feel that the failure of their parent's marriage was entirely or partially due to their wrongdoing.

I always tried to remember that I was mentoring Persephone to live the life that she would choose for herself. I wanted her to be a happy and productive adult, but she did not have to follow in my footsteps or fulfill my own lost childhood dreams.

"If living vicariously through your children is one extreme, being completely hands-off regarding how they spend their time can be equally harmful."

Let Them Star in Their Own Movie

Though we do not want to steer our children into activities and careers to fulfill our own desires, we are responsible to give them guidance. If living vicariously through your children is one extreme, being completely hands-off regarding how they spend their time can be equally harmful. Boredom is one of the biggest contributors to out-of-control emotions. Children with nothing to do must find some way to stir up excitement. Bored children who have not developed any talents or interests will find ways to fill their time, most of them useless and some of them destructive.

So how do we guide our children without overpowering them? I believe the answer lies in watching for signs of initiative on their part, so you can encourage them. This is very similar to what a good boss does. No one would say that a manager is responsible to map out the careers of his direct reports. However, he or she should be paying enough attention to note employees' talents, abilities, interests and passions.

Smart employers nurture and encourage these qualities for the good of the company and the individual. The more astute managers will tailor positions to match a valued employee's talents and interests. This grants the individual ownership of his domain in the workplace and allows him to be creative. Creativity always feels like freedom of expression, and when you combine it with passion, job satisfaction and personal fulfillment are inevitable. In so doing, employers become the primary beneficiaries.

When our interests are properly channeled, we feel motivated, empowered and rewarded. When we are truly empowered, we have multiple alternatives to accomplish a specific task, coupled with the knowledge to carefully consider all available choices and the ability to select the most suitable option. As comedian Chris Rock recently told CBS's Harry Smith, "Being rich is not about having a lot of money. Being rich is about having lots of options!"

"Being rich is not about having a lot of money. Being rich is about having lots of options!"

The same goes for our children. During their earlier years, it is best to expose them to a variety of activities—music lessons, sports, art—to give them as diverse an assortment of experiences as you are able to provide and they are able to process. Pay particular attention to schoolwork, including where your child seems to excel. Remember, you're not trying to narrow him down too early; you're just looking for clues to activities and pursuits he may enjoy. A child who is engaged in activities that interest her and give her a sense of accomplishment will not be as prone to moody episodes, because she will likely use the same activities as her creative and emotional outlet.

Two last words of caution: First, be careful not to over schedule your child. Some children are extremely high energy and need to be occupied from dawn until dusk. Others need more quiet time to reflect, draw, write or think. Be aware of this and try to accommodate your child's needs to the best of your abilities. Second, you must allow your child choices. Allow him room to fail, and room to experience and enjoy activities even when he isn't the best. Maybe your son isn't the fastest swimmer, but he loves being on a team. Foster an environment that encourages him to investigate other interests.

Remember that over time, pursued interests become habits. Good habits fueled by gratification may become passions, which, when coupled with aptitude, will become a great source of enjoyment in a person's life.

"Remember that over time, pursued interests become habits. Good habits fueled by gratification may become passions, which, when coupled with aptitude, will become a great source of enjoyment in a person's life."

If your daughter begs to take dance lessons and then ends up hating them, don't scold her as long as she gives them a fair try. But you may be less flexible if she "hates" dance because she failed to commit to the activity for a reasonable time. At work, I worry about an employee who never seems to make mistakes because it tells me that he may not be taking risks out of fear of failure of negative repercussions, thus depriving himself of all out-of-the-box thinking. I encourage my people not only to think outside the box, but also to preferably forget the shape and likeness of any cubed structure. Our children need to feel comfortable taking risks and trying new things. Our families can be that safe place where they feel free to test their wings.

The Bee in Your Bonnet

Everyone knows that once those hormones start coursing through your children's veins, there will be mood swings, which hit a fever pitch during the teen years. It is a fact of life. That does not mean life has to be enslaved to such moods, but it does mean that you are better off if you can prepare for them.

This is one of those areas where I tried the conventional wisdom, and it failed me. When Persephone was moody as a young teen, I would sit down with her sympathetically and ask her to tell me what was wrong. "Nothing," with a little sniff was nearly always the answer. I got nowhere, no matter how nicely I asked or how patiently I waited. She would stay moody, and I would grow frustrated.

Finally, I decided to make one of those tactical adjustments we discussed earlier in the book. I took a page out of Bill Cosby's playbook. Persephone and I developed a humorous way of acknowledging the obvious emotional tension without taking it too seriously. I called it the "bee in your bonnet." I used to tell her—with a smile—that if there was a bee in her bonnet, it was in her best interests to get it out before it stung her. There were two ways to deal with it: We could try to get the bee with a rolled-up newspaper (argue), or she could simply take off her bonnet and release it (let the issue go).

Underlying this little joke was the understanding that one family member is not allowed to ruin everyone else's day with a nasty mood. Certainly, we all have our ups and downs, at work as well as in our relationships. Yet it is the essence of selfishness to think that because we are in an emotionally unpleasant state, we have the right to bring everyone down. Although we don't expect the same level of maturity in children as we do in professional adults, we can and must teach them to be considerate of others and that lack of such consideration will be repaid in kind.

"It is the essence of selfishness to think that because we are in an emotionally unpleasant state, we have the right to bring everyone down."

In the process of dealing with natural teenage mood swings this way, Persephone learned to own her emotional state. She learned that while you can't always control how you feel about something, you don't have to allow that emotion to control you. You can take a deep breath, take off your "bonnet" and let the bee go. What a valuable skill for all people, young and old, to learn!

When You Are Wrong

One of the biggest myths of leadership is that the leader never has to admit fault or wrongdoing; doing so compromises his authority. We see this modeled out in the media regularly. A press secretary or some lower-level department head will come out and talk to the media or read a statement, while the CEO stays comfortably up in his executive office watching the event unfold on television.

"Real leaders understand that the authority to make decisions comes with the responsibility for the outcome when those decisions are wrong. The buck must stop with you. There can be no exception."

Real leaders understand that the authority to make decisions comes with the responsibility for the outcome when those decisions are wrong. The buck must stop with you. There can be no exception. When a leader actively accepts this responsibility, it fosters confidence among the ranks. Employees know that if something goes wrong when they are following their leader's direction, they will not be thrown under the bus.

It bears repeating that if you can foster a similar confidence in your child, you will be amazed what it will do for your relationship. The formula is simple. If you find yourself at fault, admit it. Apologize. Tell the child, "I was wrong," no matter how hard those words are to utter. Not only are you admitting that you're not infallible, but also human just like he or she is. By example, you are teaching your child that it is honorable to admit mistakes. This is the essence of accountability; actions have consequences, but it is acceptable to make a mistake as long as you proactively take responsibility for it. If your son owns his mistakes, he will undoubtedly learn valuable lessons from them.

Living in Harmony

I do not like having lots of rules at work or at home. I prefer a few basic rules that are very clear and strictly enforced. The more mature people are, the more they can infer the correct behavior from the few rules that have been articulated. For example, if the rule is "Treat others with respect," there should be no need for another rule that says "Do not stomp out of the room and slam your door."

While this is a reasonable expectation from adults, once in a while children need the corollaries of the rules spelled out. This process does not have to result in a fight, but it must be guided by the courage of your parental convictions.

Persephone went through a phase in which she would run to her room and slam her door when I told her something she did not want to hear. I told her this was unacceptable behavior, to no effect. I explained that I had no problem with her wanting to go to her room when she was annoyed with me, as I often wished I could go to mine when I was annoyed with her. As long as I knew she was safe, she was certainly allowed to be angry with me.

The door-slamming, however, made our house an unpleasant place to live, which was unfair to both of us. I told her that the next time she slammed the door I was going to remove it for a while. Unable to help herself, or simply testing the seriousness of my admonishment, she did it again. Within an hour I had removed her door from its hinges. It stayed off for a week, and she hated every minute of it. This must have made my point effectively, because I never heard another door slam again.

"When we, as parents, treat our children with courtesy and respect, we teach them to respect us, but more important, we also teach them to respect themselves."

Relationships rarely fall apart because of big issues. It is often the seemingly minor acts of disrespect and disregard that eventually inflict deep wounds on our hearts. On the other hand, little daily courtesies have the power to bind us together in love and trust. When we, as parents, treat our children with courtesy and respect, we teach them to respect us, but more important, we also teach them to respect themselves.

I was always conscious that the way I treated Persephone would shape her thinking of how men ought to treat her. While chivalry may be a dying art, I have always thought it proper for men to open doors for women and offer other such courtesies. Naturally there came a day during her early teenage years when she told me she could open her own car door.

"This is not about you being able to open the door," I explained. "This is about me wanting to open the door for you." By the time she was in high school, I heard her tell a boyfriend that her dad always opened the door for her. The next time I saw the boyfriend, he was opening the door for Persephone. Years later I smiled when I saw Eduardo, a fine young man who is soon to be my son-in-law, open the car door for her as they were leaving our home. She noticed me smiling with satisfaction and answered me with a wink. That's my girl!

There has never been a doubt in my mind that my daughter can open her own door, as well as achieve anything else to which she puts her mind. What I have been pleased to see is that as I have strived to teach her to treat others with courtesy and respect, she has learned to expect courteous and respectful treatment for herself. Neither she nor I will ever be willing to settle for anything less.

"I have been pleased to see that as I have strived to teach her to treat others with courtesy and respect, she has learned to expect courteous and respectful treatment for herself."

"Motivated professionals know that it is all too easy to let work consume your entire life, even when your family is in absolutely no danger of physical starvation."

CHAPTER 8

THE BALANCING ACT

AN AMERICAN TOURIST AND HIS TEENAGE SON were visiting a small town in Central America where people still washed their clothes in the river and carried them up a large hill to dry on the sun-soaked grass. The men watched as two small grandmothers carried huge baskets of wet clothes on their heads from the riverbank to the hill. Desiring to be chivalrous, they offered to carry the baskets. The women smiled kindly and offered them their loads. To their shock, the men found that they could barely lift the baskets, let alone lug them up the hill. Embarrassed, they watched the women return the clothes to their heads with ease and finish their journey.

The women in this story were not stronger than the two men who wanted to help them. They had perfected the art of harnessing the strength of their entire bodies to greater ends by keeping their loads perfectly in balance. Our lives can be much the same way. We are all given 24 hours in a day. We all have to make a living and raise our children at the same time. Yet some of us are able to make much better use of this time than others.

I am not for a moment expressing lack of sympathy for those who struggle to both put food on the table and spend quality time with their children. They have always been my heroes and have my utmost respect. But the fact remains that motivated professionals know that it is all too easy to let work consume your entire life, even when your family is in absolutely no danger of physical starvation.

Both work and family require our energy and attention. How can we balance the load? I will attempt to offer you some principles, rather than specific instructions. Ultimately, families are as unique as individuals, with different specific issues at play in each case. Yet when we have our priorities aligned properly, the daily decisions of how to spend each moment will become much simpler.

"I have always found the notion that all we owe our children is a roof over their heads, food on the table, and clothes on their backs to be outrageous. These are nothing but the 'basic requirements,' a parent's minimum obligation."

Going Above and Beyond

Early in my career I hired a talented and bright employee, freshly graduated from a major university. During the job interview, I had inquired about her salary requirements. When I offered her the position, it was with a salary 20 percent higher than she had requested. This was not an act of generosity, but a wise business move.

I knew that her talent would be just as obvious to other employers as it was to me. I needed to give her ample reason to stay with our company so we would not train her only to lose her a year later when she realized that she could command a higher salary. I have made similar offers on other occasions for the same reasons.

In the same way, the world is full of influences that would love to raise our children for us. Peer groups, popular culture, or even other institutions clamor for our children's attention and loyalty. If we hope to keep them, we must invest more than the "basic requirements."

There is something particularly sacred about a parent's obligation to his or her child. After all, our children did not ask to be born. We brought them into this world and so we owe them a good upbringing. I have always found the notion that all we owe our children is a roof over their heads, food on the table, and clothes on their backs to be outrageous. These are nothing but the "basic requirements," a parent's minimum obligation. We parents must strive to far exceed the basic requirements. If we truly value our children, we will invest in them. Although money is part of this investment, the most precious investment we can make is our time and attention.

The Art of Being There

Everyone's time is limited. However, a creative parent can include his children in his life in a way that will further the mentoring relationship. When Persephone was younger, for example, she accompanied me on a few car-shopping expeditions. She listened intently as I discussed with her what we were going to do and how we were going to do it. Once at the dealership, she observed me with great interest as I set certain parameters, established my bottom line, negotiated and successfully pursued the deal I had envisioned before ever entering the car dealer's lot. She saw firsthand that negotiating is an art of give and take, and that a price tag or a first offer is rarely etched in stone.

Years later when we were shopping for her car, she designed a similar deal and negotiated it in part while I took care of the finances. Not long ago, Persephone was able to walk into that same dealership on her own credit and negotiate for her own car just as she had seen me do. The original car-shopping trip was something I had to do anyway, but, by including her, I was not only buying a car, I was teaching my daughter an important life skill. Including our children in activities like this—even if they are not initially enthusiastic about it—lets them know they are an integral part of our lives whose physical, emotional and intellectual presence we deeply value.

"A creative parent can include his children in his life in a way that will further the mentoring relationship."

I have talked to parents who rationalize their lack of quality time with their children by pointing out the many parents who are forced to spend months away, such as members of the military and other professions that require heavy travel. My heart goes out to parents who are forced to miss important holidays, birthdays and other precious moments with their families. Yet my view has always been that this should cause us to treasure and prioritize our time with our children all the more. If we have the power to be there, we should be there.

Every human being has the desire to feel special. In particular children need to feel special to their parents. Remember, children crave our approval. When I was in high school, at the last minute I was chosen to be the flag bearer in a parade. I was shocked and overjoyed at the opportunity, because this position was always reserved for the best student in the class, and while I was reasonably good, I was not the best. A team of 50-plus classmates would be following me as we marched through the main streets of the city in front of everyone. It was a wonderful experience, but my parents were unable to share it with me because they were on a rare out-of-town trip.

They had never missed anything of importance to all of us before. They were always there. While I intellectually understood their reasons, I still was profoundly disappointed.

As an adult, there were two ways I could interpret this childhood experience. I could say to myself, "Well, my parents missed a big moment in my life, and I was fine. I don't blame them, and we have a great relationship to this day." Or I could remember what it felt like to be that young man and say, "I don't want my child to feel that sense of disappointment if there is anything I can do to avoid it. I will do everything in my power to be there for Persephone when she needs me."

Two weeks before her third birthday, I had the opportunity to decide which approach I would take. I was on a 10-day business trip to Europe, set to return on a Sunday when our church had organized a Halloween pageant for all the little kids. My daughter was going to be dressed up as an angel marching around the church just as I had marched as the flag bearer so many years ago. Like my parents, I had a very reasonable excuse to miss the event. I was scheduled to fly from Lisbon to JFK, but my connecting flight would not arrive in Washington until 6:30. The pageant started at 5:00.

As the trip drew to a close the fact that I would miss my daughter's first performance weighed heavily on my heart. My last evening in Europe, I picked up the phone and called the airline. I rearranged my schedule with a series of complicated connections that allowed me to land in Washington at 4:00. I knew I still needed all the stars to align perfectly to make the show, but I also knew I was doing my absolute best to be there for her.

I raced off my plane, passed baggage claim and hailed a cab. I walked into the church hall five minutes before Persephone was due onstage. I had not told anyone of my plans to be there because I wasn't sure if I would make it. Yet the moment she appeared in front of the crowd, her eyes scanned the room and found me in the back. Her face lit up and she waved to me excitedly with both hands. Any jetlag or fatigue I might have been feeling disappeared at that moment, and my heart was overwhelmed with joy. It was then I realized that this was not just something I had done because it was best for my daughter: *It was the best thing for me.*

It is easy to forget in the midst of meetings and deadlines the indescribable joy our children can bring us in those special moments. In the years that followed, there were many occasions when my commitment to be there for Persephone took a fair amount of sacrifice. I had to rearrange business commitments or adjust my workload so I could leave in the middle of the workday for a school play that began at 3:30 in the afternoon. As she grew older, she knew that if she wanted me there, she had to let me know about the event as soon as she found out. As I prioritized her schedule, I required that she respect mine, and she did.

All Grown Up?

Parents of teenagers often assume that their children have outgrown their need for parental presence. Yet I found the opposite to be true. Persephone was involved in a sorority in college, and she asked me to attend an event one Saturday afternoon. I went to the function and I was the only parent there. It didn't bother me in the least, and it clearly did not bother her. The day she graduated she gave me a card thanking me for a number of things I had done for her. My presence at that sorority event made the list.

5/17/09

persephone's
Thank you's

*Thank you for...
1) moving me in on my 1st day of school + comforting me through all my fears
2) visiting UMiami + FSU, because I was so eager to leave
3) taking me to Greece w/ xxxx even though I know you didn't like him
4) taking Tara + I on our 1st cruise - it's still talked about to this day
5) letting my focus on my grades instead of working through school
6) wiring the cable for the TV in my trailer park dorm room
7) never missing a moment... ever
8) letting me move into a townhouse even though I was a sophomore
9) letting me join AOΠ - it was one of the best decisions I made in college + completely changed my experience
10) donating $ to AOΠ
11) offering to hire me because it would look better on my resume + pay more than Coastal Fights

12) Listening to me everytime I felt down or conflicted. You were always there to lift me up + guide me

13) being at Greek bang even though you were the only parent there

14) your support even though you hated my bf - you were watching out for me

15) letting me plan your b-day party. to this day that was one of the best nights of my life.

16) your support during recruitment for 2 years

17) pushing me to study abroad - I've never had a better time in my life or grown so much in such a short period of time

18) threatening him because he sucked + you made me realize it

19) "dropping me off" with J in London - I would've never been ok without you there

20) realizing how awesome Eddie is- your approval means everything

21) bringing Christmas lights to AOT recruitment

22) being at my Betta Gamma Sigma ceremony

23) marrying Jules- she's one of the best things to ever happen to you and therefore one of the best things to happen to me

24) giving me a 21st bday on a yacht!

25) coming into my negotiations class despite my initial reluctance

26) always being proud everytime I called to tell you
a Grace

persephone

27) laughing at every drunk dial

28) singing + dancing with me at Jimmy Buffett

29) your support no matter what

30) just being you - I can only pray that I marry someone that will be 1/2 the father you have been to me!

Love you forever,

Joseph

PS Thank you for the graduation necklace, party + dinner! I love you!

There were other times when a younger Persephone needed to know that she was the most important person in my life. I remember being driven to a meeting in Bangkok when I received a call on my cell phone. I could tell something was bothering my daughter. I asked her to give me two minutes and call me back. I immediately postponed the meeting for an hour and took the time to listen to her. The call probably cost about $500, but it did matter. I rationalized it as part of the cost of doing business.

"I was always there for her when it was within my power."

To be honest, I cannot even remember what the problem was. What was important was that Persephone knew, no matter what I had to do for work, she was my priority. Of course there would be times I couldn't rearrange the meeting. There are wonderful parents who do not own the company they work for and can't call the shots the way I was able to do. The important issue was that I was always there for her *when it was within my power*. I tried to hold true to that commitment, whether I was preparing for a meeting, at home, or in a car somewhere in Thailand, and I never discussed it with her to make her feel obligated to offer something in return. I have always believed that parents' offerings must be unconditional, never quid pro quo.

> *"We expect a good mother to be there for her children, even if she has a full-time job outside the home. Yet my experience with my daughter's friends showed me that we have significantly lower expectations of fathers."*

"Absent" Fathers

I realize that there are many parents, mothers in particular, who do exactly what I have described above. We expect a good mother to be there for her children, even if she has a full-time job outside the home. Yet my experience with my daughter's friends showed me that we have significantly lower expectations of fathers.

Through the years, many of Persephone's friends were not only surprised by my presence at various events, but also by how comfortable she was with me there. They were initially timid around me, not really knowing how to speak or relate to me. In an effort to put them at ease, I would always try to chat with them. It was hard work, but I persisted, feeling that it was important to get to know my daughter's friends. I also wanted them to get to know me and to be comfortable in our home, because I much preferred them over at our house than out somewhere unsupervised.

What I found was that I actually began to establish meaningful relationships with Persephone's friends. They were great kids, and I enjoyed getting to know them; in fact to this day many of them refer to me as Papa E. I wondered why they found my interest in them as people so surprising. What I realized, time and time again, was that they saw fathers as intimidating, aloof, disconnected figures to whom they could not relate. My willingness to invest time and energy with my daughter ultimately allowed me to be an influence on her friends as well.

One of Persephone's friends, in particular, became almost like a surrogate daughter to me. Tara traveled with us to Greece, and my family there treated her as if she were Persephone's sister. On August 1, 2005, days before Tara left home to start her freshman year in college, she came to the house to say goodbye. I was not there, but she left for me a lovely silver keychain with an airplane on one end and a globe on the other, along with a poem she wrote to me, which appears on the following pages.

Few things have moved me more deeply or given me greater satisfaction. Since that day, I have used the key chain each day I enter my office, and I look at her poem hanging on the wall over my desk, a humble reminder that I somehow had the good fortune to influence another young life.

Tara is getting married in the fall. She recently asked me to be a reader at her wedding. I am humbled and at a loss for words at her gesture. It is difficult for me to comprehend such enormous gratitude on her part for doing nothing more than I did for my own daughter, but it is a testament to the footprint one can leave in a young child's life.

I Just Want To Say...
Thank You

They say that actions speak a thousand words,
and a smile brings us light.
They say love will bring us wonders,
and push our fears out of sight.
I am to believe in second chances,
and some have come my way.
I have had many prayers answered,
even on the worst of my days.
I have cried on countless occasions,
and have broken into two,
I've been taught the hardest lessons,
which I learned early in my youth.
I have been given opportunity,
I made the choice to take a chance,
not knowing if this look at life,
would be my one last glance.
I have awoken every morning,
for the light brings a new day,
and when the sun starts setting,
I just dream my life away.
I don't dream of unknown places,
or where I'll be when I'm not here,
I don't dream of life after death,
and when the time is near.
My dreams are re-lived moments,
they make me smile in my sleep,
and when my dream is over,
it's another moment I shall keep.
I awaken with a smile,
and a thankful breath of air,
and walk over to my window,
to thank the man upstairs.
I was living in a fantasy,
I thought it was a dream,
I thought for sure, if I blinked an eye,
it wouldn't be what it seemed.

But the next day was the same feeling,
it brought tears to my eyes,
I was given the chance to look at the man,
who was my angel in disguise.
The moments were not temporary,
they became my way life,
I left my darkened days behind,
and ended all my strife's.
I was handed a god-given gift,
a soul mate made of gold,
A reason to smile through my days,
and a story to be told.
My life had new meaning,
and my prayers must have been heard,
because I can't explain this feeling,
I just can't find the words.
The time just kept on ticking,
it was a month, and now its years,
of memories I will forever cherish,
I'll look back with laugh and tears.
I was given opportunities,
I never imagined I would see,
I flew across the ocean,
with my best friend next to me.
I traveled to the city,
and walked along the beach,
I watched the most beautiful sun I've ever seen,
set way beyond my reach.
I have experienced my ups and downs,
and could not have made it through,
the roughest waves, and toughest battles,
if it had not been for you.
Your actions have spoken a million words,
you have given me my light;
you have delivered me my second chance,
you have taught me wrong from right.
You are to me, more than family,
you are my angel in disguise,
your warmth, your love, and caring ways,
forever bring tears to my eyes.

I just want to say thank you,
for giving me your hand,
and guiding me through this thing called life,
as change starts to take a stand.
I just want to say thank you,
for always taking the time,
to show me how things can really be,
when there are too many mountains to climb.
I just want to say thank you,
for teaching the unknown,
and for all the countless times
that you opened up your home.
I just want to say thank you,
for being the father I never had,
for filling the shoes of a man,
I'm ashamed to call my Dad.
I just want to say thank you,
for the daughter that you raise,
for the moments you have given us,
and the unforgettable days.
I just want to say thank you,
for always helping me,
you have made me the person I am today,
and have showed me who I can really be.
I just want to say thank you,
I don't think you'll ever know,
how thankful I am that you're a part of my life,
and how much you've helped me grow.

Papa E.

Just a little something to let
you know how much i
appreciate everything
you have done for me.
Thank you Papa E. i ♡ u.
always, Tara

> *"Think about the parent that you want to be and decide what you are willing to sacrifice to become that person."*

Finding the Balance

Those women who balanced the baskets of clothes on their heads had to be able to adjust their loads with speed and agility as they made their way up the hill. In our lives, we must be willing to evaluate and adjust how we spend our time if we are to keep our priorities aligned in the face of daily challenges.

Think about the parent that you want to be and decide what you are willing to sacrifice to become that person. Realize that just as sure as you cannot be in two places at once, you cannot be everything to everybody. Instead, determine to be the best person you can be to the people who are most important to you.

The rewards for investing time in our children are both immediate – the surge of joy we feel in the moment – and long-term. When our children grow up, they will probably not remember what our business title was, how many people reported to us, how fast we ascended the corporate ladder, or how much money our company made each year. They will most likely remember however, that piano recital or that soccer game where they looked up and saw our faces, smiling at them. Remember that, and do all in your power to be there. If you cannot be there physically, be there emotionally. There is no excuse for falling short of that mark!

CHAPTER 9

―――――∽―――――

BUILDING YOUR TEAM

ALL SENSIBLE MANAGERS KNOW THAT THEY HAVE TO cultivate some spirit of camaraderie and shared interests among their employees. Countless books have been written about building an effective team at the office, prompting managers to plan retreats, fund social activities, and craft mission statements. Why would we expect our children to require less effort?

Staying Close

A truth I learned from running my company is that physical proximity does not necessarily translate into relational connectedness. Just because everyone works under the same roof doesn't mean they share the company's vision, goals and values. The same goes for families. We can all live together, but lead entirely separate lives.

On the other hand, physical distance does not have to mean a distant relationship. Only four of my employees live in the same metro region as our office. Everyone else works remotely, and we're connected electronically to other continents. Yet with consistent, quality communication, our tasks are completed on time as a team.

When I came to this country at 18, I left behind my parents, a 14-year-old sister and a 5-year-old brother. I never feared that the physical distance would damage our close relationship, and I am happy to say that it did not. Living on different continents for 35 years, we are closer today than we have ever been, and our children share the same closeness. Of course, like everything worth cherishing, emotional intimacy requires effort to cultivate and maintain. We did the work, and as a result, our relationships have thrived even though we have not lived under the same roof for all these years.

> *"We cannot assume the kids feel like "part of a team" just because we are sharing living quarters."*

It should be clear from my examples in the last chapter that I am not suggesting parents spend long periods of time away from their children unless it is absolutely necessary. I am saying that no matter how often we are in the same room with our children, as parents we must pay special attention to the consistency and quality of our communication. We cannot assume the kids feel like "part of a team" just because we are sharing living quarters.

> *"We can never expect team members to invest in the team more than we do. On the other hand, when a team leader—CDO or CEO—invests heavily in the team, the members will follow suit."*

Investing in the Team

We can never expect team members to invest in the team more than we do. On the other hand, when a team leader—CDO or CEO—invests heavily in the team, the members will follow suit. My silent commitment to both my employees and myself has always been that I will never dismiss anyone because I don't have enough work to support them. During a recent economic downturn that put many companies out of business, I invested heavily in the company and aggressively raised capital from investors to avoid layoffs.

Still, our company got to a difficult point, and my board concluded we could address this through layoffs, furloughs or salary deferments. I insisted we move forward with one salary deferment: mine. I didn't make a big deal about this; I simply told my team that I was putting good money into the company, and tangibly proved to them that I believed we would succeed.

Their response overwhelmed me. Though I had never asked for any concessions, employees came forward and offered part of their own salaries back to the company. I received a return on my investment in the company many times over by the loyalty, understanding, respect, and the undying commitment of my people. None of us welcomed that adversity, but in it I proved to them that I was fully committed to the company and the team, and they repaid me in kind.

Three months later, opportunities I had been cultivating came to fruition, and I was able to pay myself again. Years later, we are still in business and doing well. All of those people who went through that season with me are still with me today and will be with the company for as long as they desire.

How can we prove to our children that we are invested in our families? The answer may look different for different people. I have already detailed many ways I demonstrated my investment in Persephone over the years. When I had to be at work, she knew that I was earning money to take care of her. The challenge presented by my divorce enabled me to prove my commitment to her at another level.

Even when Persephone was being punished, I made sure she understood that it was for her own good and it brought me no pleasure. Imposing our will on our children certainly keeps them under control in the short term, but it builds no loyalty. We must help them understand that part of being on a team is playing by the rules, and the same rules must apply to all appropriately.

"The value of a victory is always based on the quality of the competition. You can win a match with a weaker opponent, but that would be akin to a mature adult arm-wrestling a baby. There is no glory, satisfaction or self-respect when the match is over."

Cultivating Win-Win Solutions

Competition is a natural instinct at home and a work, but a good leader finds ways to cultivate win-win outcomes. Early in my career, I found myself in a two-week training course about new products our company was marketing to physicians. Marketing to such an educated group meant we were forced to learn reams of information practically overnight. One's performance during such training could make or break a career, and naturally, some did better than others.

In this case, my classmates were my competition, and my roommate during this training period was particularly sharp. There were two ways I could have approached this reality. I could have worked to undermine my competitors by withholding information, trickery and deceit, or I could help create a higher tide that would raise all boats. The latter approach suited me best. My roommate and I supported one another. During group exercises, I chose to share information that helped the class as a whole. This was a risky strategy, but I wanted to succeed as a gentleman, not a scoundrel. After all, the value of a victory is always based on the quality of the competition. You can win a match with a weaker opponent, but that would be akin to a mature adult arm-wrestling a baby. There is no glory, satisfaction or self-respect when the match is over.

"Togetherness among family members does not come from sharing DNA. It is nurtured by hard work and leading by example."

My gamble paid off. At the end of the two weeks, the trainers saw fit to award me the Outstanding Trainee award and the Outstanding Peer Influencer award. More than 25 years have passed since that day and as of this writing, I'm the only person to have received both awards from this course. The executives took notice, and that evening changed my career forever.

We can cultivate the same kind of win-win scenarios at home. While my parenting experience has been with an only child, I am blessed to be married to a woman who raised three daughters on her own before marrying me. I learned from her that the key to avoiding unhealthy competition between family members is for all children to know that regardless of performance, they are equally loved.

Reward and affirm the behavior you want. When your children help one another and work together well, let them know that you notice. You don't have to give out an "Outstanding Sibling Influencer" award, but you can tell your daughter, "I really appreciate how you helped your brother with his homework. You are such a good example to him," or your son, "Good job teaching your sister to ride her bike. She wants to be just like you."

Siblings do not have to fight all the time. Some conflict is clearly inevitable, but their relationships will be modeled on what they see in you. If you are cold, selfish and competitive to a fault, they will follow suit or, worse, dismiss you. If they see you generous with your time and attention, they will help and encourage each other, even if they occasionally argue. Togetherness among family members does not come from sharing DNA. It is nurtured by hard work and leading by example.

Teaching Teamwork

I learned extremely valuable teamwork lessons when I was a product manager. Early on, I realized that I was the hub of a very complicated wheel. My duties required that I interact with all different departments and specialists within those departments, from sales to manufacturing. There was no direct reporting responsibility with any of them, but if production didn't meet my desired schedule, I'd have nothing to market. In short, I wasn't in charge of anyone, but I needed everyone doing their jobs well in order to do mine.

This lesson in humility and interdependence served me, and later my wife Juliana, very well in our life together. All children tend to think they know more than they actually do. When Persephone was planning my 50th birthday party, she wanted to do it all by herself. Her stepmom-to-be didn't compete with her, but gently offered good suggestions. Persephone initially resisted, but soon realized the party was a bigger task than she originally anticipated. Why turn down good help?

While Juliana hadn't known me as long as my daughter, she was a mature adult with lots of wisdom and experience. She didn't care about getting credit for her ideas or suggestions; she just wanted to help her future stepdaughter reach her goal. As a team, they threw me the best birthday party anyone could have asked for, and in the process they grew closer together by supporting each other every step of the way and delighting in the outcome.

Building Trust

No team can function effectively without trust. This is true between employees and management, companies and their customers, and definitely between parents and children. As parents, we are only as strong as our word. A wise man once said it is better not to promise than to break your promise. In business, we call it under-promising but over-delivering.

Children have amazing memories, especially for the things we promise. They experience profound disappointment when we don't follow through on our word. The best way to guard against broken promises is to think very carefully before you speak. A good salesperson wouldn't promise a valued customer something he couldn't deliver; treat your children with the same courtesy and respect.

"A good sales-person wouldn't promise a valued customer something he couldn't deliver; treat your children with the same courtesy and respect."

When Persephone's mother and I were divorcing, it was very important to her that I pick her up for our visits when I said I would. She would call me every time I was to get her and ask me what time I was going to be there. I made it a point to be punctual to the minute, oftentimes arriving in the neighborhood early and waiting in the car. It almost became our little game. Games aside, I was really proving to her that I was reliable, and that she could count on me. When Persephone was almost 9 years old, she acknowledged her trust in me in a note she wrote during Fathers' Visiting Day at her school.

He loves Golf!

My dad is my best friend in the
whole wide world. I like when
we go to fun places together.
My dad has his own business
called "Cogent." I think that is
an awesome name. My dad's name
is Chris ~~Effina~~. And for a
living he teaches doctors
and makes C.D. Romes. I
also like him because I
can trust him the most.
He loves hot things to
eat. He loves the Macrena
even though he tells me
"That is the stupedist
song." I think he is a
cool dad.

Norwood
School
Visting.
Day

11/8/96

Kids are also like customers in that they are really not interested in excuses. They don't care why you were late or what happened to prevent you from taking them to the baseball game. They just know you didn't do what you said you would. This doesn't mean you'll never break a promise; it just means you need to take it seriously and apologize sincerely when you do.

When the Team Breaks Up

How hiring and firing is handled in a company sends a message to all the employees about what it means to be part of the team. In the same way, the way your marriage is handled will send strong messages to your children about what it means to be part of your family. This is why so many children of divorce struggle with fear and self-esteem issues. However, I am pleased to say that while divorce is never ideal, it does not have to destroy your family's team.

Disappointment—whether a failed marriage or a failed company—can feel debilitating. It is so easy to become paralyzed and rendered unable to ever give it another try. Once again, the business world had lessons for me in my home life. Early in my career an employer and I had an ethical disagreement. I was young and I needed the job, but I submitted a letter of resignation rather than sully my reputation by doing what my bosses wanted me to do. In my youthful naiveté, I thought he would understand, and even sympathize. Instead he reacted with rage, telling me in effect, "You can't quit—you're fired."

I had my integrity, but I needed a job. So in the face of very pressing circumstances I started my first company. I had just mailed my first mortgage check for a new house. My family was depending on me to provide for them. Rather than yield to paralysis, I took responsibility for my decision. I took everything I had learned at my previous job, combined it with the recent hard-learned lessons on ethics and morals, and poured it into making my own company all it could be.

Marriage is the ultimate partnership enterprise, and when it fails, it's never just one person's fault. It is very tempting to just gloss over the unfortunate occurrence in the name of "moving on," but I knew I had to accept responsibility for my part. Blaming Persephone's mother entirely would have not only been unfair, it would have been making excuses for my own shortcomings.

There are two dangers to avoid with divorce. If we treat it lightly, we send the message that family commitments are not a big deal. On the other hand, treating it like the end of the world is like telling our children our family is somehow incomplete or defective. For me, the key was to face the reality of my broken first marriage and show Persephone that better days lay ahead. My willingness to accept responsibility for my side also showed Persephone not to fear failure. When I was fortunate enough to meet Juliana, I was prepared to try anew, having learned from my past mistakes.

"Moral courage is one of the rarest commodities of our day. To be cohesive, a team must know what it stands for."

What Does Your Team Stand For?

"The darkest places in hell," Dante said, "are reserved for those who maintain their neutrality in times of moral crisis." Moral courage is one of the rarest commodities of our day. To be cohesive, a team must know what it stands for. As a leader, if you do not have the courage of deep moral convictions, you have nothing to rally your family behind. Your children should know the values of your family and embrace them as their own.

Convictions come with a price. You must not be afraid to stick your neck out, lose friends, or even sacrifice financially. But when you have learned how to do this, the rewards you reap in your children are amazing. Persephone grew up knowing that one of my most treasured values was helping those less fortunate than I, without taking credit.

"Some people only give to be congratulated, but pure generosity never needs public recognition."

She saw me giving money to homeless people, and questioned why I did it. I would explain. She knew that I gave money to certain projects without wanting my name attached to it. I explained some people only give to be congratulated, but pure generosity never needs public recognition. I had always sought to instill this value in her, but I never wanted to force her to participate, because coerced charity is no charity at all.

Persephone was a freshman in college when Hurricane Katrina devastated the Gulf Coast of the United States, and she was immediately moved to get involved. Without breathing much of a word to anyone, she got permission from the dean of students to set up collection buckets on campus for donations. She recruited volunteers under the banner "Spare Change for Change," and before the week was out she had collected more than $1,000 for the Red Cross relief efforts. Although the event became the most high-profile student-generated relief effort at her college, her name was nowhere to be found. She organized it because it was in her heart, not to get credit or beef up her resume.

What I love about that kind of giving is that it takes authentic self-confidence. When you truly know who you are, you don't need others to tell you you're great. Ultimately, to raise independent and responsible adults, we must teach our children who they are. They are part of a team, a family and a community, all of which stand for certain values. Whatever your specific beliefs, they must guide you in times of moral challenge to do the good, honest and courageous thing. Then your team will have someone worthy to follow, because true leadership is built on a foundation of care and compassion for all.

"Every venture has a bottom line. In parenting, it is raising a responsible, independent adult who still not only wants, but also cherishes, a relationship with you."

CHAPTER 10

THE BOTTOM LINE

EVERY VENTURE HAS A BOTTOM LINE. In football or soccer, it is winning more games. In business, it is increasing profits. In parenting, it is raising a responsible, independent adult who still not only wants, but also cherishes, a relationship with you.

Naturally, the journey along the way is at least as important as the destination. Do you feel like you gave it your all? Does your business enjoy a good reputation? Are you enjoying your children as they grow up? Yet in all these areas, if you lose sight of your bottom line, you run the risk of going astray. Life is full of distractions; every day we must make the effort to stay focused on what is most important.

"To achieve our bottom line goals with our children, we must teach them that they do not need to do anything unwise to be special or conform thoughtlessly to earn acceptance."

Learning to Lead

None of us wants our children to be members of the herd, moving thoughtlessly with every trend or whim. So how do we teach them to lead? First we teach them that we value them as individuals and that as individuals, their power is rooted in their ability to make their own decisions.

When Persephone was 12 we visited a shopping complex, the entrance of which had a revolving door and a long line of people waiting to enter. There was a single door to the left and to the right of the revolving door that no one was using.

So I took my daughter by the hand and headed toward one of the side doors. At first she resisted, feeling we should wait along with everyone else. I assured her that everything would be fine. We entered the mall and moments later she noticed a new line forming at the very door we had used.

"That is the herd mentality," I explained, pointing to the revolving door. "They are all going very slowly to the same place by the same route. But as soon as we took a different path, what happened?"

"Other people followed," she replied.

"Exactly," I agreed. "Never be afraid to take a different path. Someone has to."

Years later, in conversation, Persephone and I would often reference that experience. "I just broke free from the herd," she would say, to explain a decision she made that was different from what everyone else was doing.

Every child needs to learn that while there are rules that must be observed, they should also question the actions of the crowd before joining in. As the old adage goes, "there's more than one way to skin a cat." The way the crowd is going may be best for you, but it may not.

The idea is not to become mired in indecision, but rather to apply a measure of thought to the process.

Children and adults have a love/hate relationship with individuality. On one hand, we all want to feel special. On the other, we all need to feel accepted. To achieve our bottom line goals with our children, we must teach them that they do not need to do anything unwise to be special or conform thoughtlessly to earn acceptance.

The Beauty of Accountability

Not long ago, one of my interns approached me with a proposal for a data gathering service. He was part of a team investigating various options for our company, and gave me a well-thought-out presentation. I appreciated his effort and was willing to give it a try.

Unfortunately, we soon discovered that the system was not working as hoped and in actuality caused a great deal of extra work. I received several calls about the situation while I was out of the country, and ultimately suggested we shut the service down and discuss it when I returned.

Persephone, now a young woman, was interning at the office at the time. The new system's failure was causing anxiety among even a few senior staff, some of whom expressed concern that I might return and fire the team that came up with the idea. Persephone told them in no uncertain terms that she would be shocked if that occurred for such a reason. They were reassured, but not convinced.

When I returned to the office, I asked the people involved to meet with me to discuss the status of the project. As they entered my office I saw fear on their faces.

"What have we done to fix the problem?" I asked. Their immediate response was to explain and defend their actions. Listening silently, I let them have their say.

Finally, I spoke again. "You are all missing the point," I said. "There was nothing wrong with suggesting a new system. There was nothing wrong with the way that you thought through the pros and cons. There is nothing wrong with anyone because I accepted your proposal. It simply didn't work out the way we thought it would, so we are shutting it down."

"Accountability is not a dirty word; it is a beautiful one. It allows us the freedom to try new things, but the constraint to learn from our mistakes."

The group stared at me in disbelief.

I continued, "What did we miss in our initial evaluation, and what have we done to fix the problem?" One by one, suggestions started coming forward. At the end of the meeting, all the team members but one had explained how they might have been more thorough researching and testing the system prior to its implementation. The team member who refused to accept my decision to shut the service down defended it as implemented, simply because it was his idea, and often blamed his teammates for the failure.

Immediately, there were two strikes against him. He refused to be accountable even when there were no repercussions for coming clean, and he tossed a few of his teammates under the bus in an effort to absolve himself. I thought it a waste of everyone's time to wait for the third strike. Two weeks later when that phase of the internship was over, he was the only person that was not asked to return to the team.

As we've discussed, Persephone knew that it was OK to make a mistake as long as you took responsibility for it. Accountability is not a dirty word; it is a beautiful one. It allows us the freedom to try new things, but the constraint to learn from our mistakes. She would carry this lesson into her own decision-making as an adult.

Protecting the Bottom Line

No one is immune to tragedy. A manager can make all the right decisions, invest in her team faithfully, and a fire can take out her entire warehouse. We cannot prevent every fire, but we can purchase insurance: a guard against something we hope will never happen. In the same way, a parent can set high standards, mentor his children in all the important life skills and one bad decision can rob him of his child's life or health.

Every year, especially around graduation time, we learn from the local news reports of too many preventable deaths of young people due to drunken driving, alcohol overdoses, or other senseless accidents. A survey of these stories shows that many of these children were headed to college, their lives full of promise. Were they all rebellious and defiant? I don't think so. Many just made one stupid mistake that ended up maiming them or even costing their lives.

To do all I could to prevent Persephone from ever being numbered among such tragedies, we had a deal. I offered a onetime get-out-of-jail-free card. I told her that even kids who are mindful of potentially troublesome circumstances sometimes find themselves in a situation where they feel uncomfortable or unsafe and need to get to safety right away. The last thing I would want in that situation is for my child not to call me because she was afraid of my reaction.

> *"I offered a onetime get-out-of-jail-free card.*
> *Our deal was that she had one chance to call me,*
> *wherever she was, whatever the time, whatever*
> *the circumstances, and whatever her condition.*
> *I would come and get her and I would never*
> *question what happened or how she got there."*

So our deal was that she had one chance to call me, wherever she was, whatever the time, whatever the circumstances, and whatever her condition. I would come and get her and I would never question what happened or how she got there. She would not be punished or experience repercussions of any kind. We would simply forget the event ever happened. It would be a far better outcome for her than the alternative.

There was, of course, one exception. I had told Persephone that in the event she were careless and ended up in jail, to expect to be sitting in a cell for at least 24 hours before I got there. All actions have consequences; carelessness is no exception.

I have already discussed why punishment is a necessary part of raising children. However, no parent wants his or her child to take a life-threatening risk out of fear of repercussions. The get-out-of-jail-free card worked for us: Persephone made it through her adolescent and young adult years safely and responsibly. She knew her physical safety and emotional wellbeing were far more precious to me than anything else, and I am happy to say she never needed to take advantage of my offer.

"Many children today only experience the use of money, while learning none of the skills needed to maintain a similar lifestyle as adults."

Financial Independence

Most mature individuals seem to manage their money responsibly. Many children today, however, only experience the use of money, while learning none of the skills needed to maintain a similar lifestyle as adults. Many parents believe that fiscal responsibility is taught by charging their children rent or mandating that they maintain a job while in school. I was never a believer in charging my child room and board or making her struggle unnecessarily, because I found that approach to be ineffective in accomplishing the stated goal. I worked closely with Persephone to ensure that she understood not only the use of money, but also the value of sound financial management. I worked to teach her the importance of managing her *cash flow*, borrowing, timely bill payment, and the enormous value of establishing and maintaining good credit.

There was a time when most college students had to ration their pocket money carefully to have enough for an ice cream soda or a movie on the weekend. When I was in college, I had a bottle where I dropped pennies every day, and once or twice a year I'd have enough for a dinner at a nice restaurant. Today's students are bombarded with offers for credit cards as soon as they arrive on campus. Many are saddled with burdensome credit card debt at ridiculous interest rates in addition to their student loans. Before these kids figure out what credit is for, they've ruined it.

"Teach your child the importance of managing her cash flow, borrowing, timely bill payment, and the enormous value of establishing and maintaining good credit."

Anyone can run a company without profit, but no one can run a company without cash. The same applies to life. We've all heard the cliché "Cash is king." I actually believe and teach that "Cash is prince," because *"Cash flow is king."*

Many young people fail to manage their cash flow properly and run out of money before the next paycheck, unable to meet their financial obligations. They miss credit card payments, car loan payments, or, worse, student loan payments. Soon threatening letters and phone calls begin, and inevitably collection notices and derogatory statements on their credit report weigh down their credit score. In some cases, young adults before the age of 30 file for personal bankruptcy and then spend a good part of their lives rehabilitating their credit. More important, prospective employers, landlords, and other credit issuers routinely check the credit score before offering employment or approving an apartment lease.

> *"We've all heard the cliché 'Cash is king.' I actually believe and teach that 'Cash is prince,' because 'Cash flow is king.' "*

Here is the problem most young kids run into. An amount of money goes to their bank account every week or every two weeks. They pay whatever bills are due at the time, and see a significant surplus remaining in the account. Most treat it as extra spending money and do exactly that. They spend it. This is the ultimate in a false sense of security, because while they think that the "surplus" is spending money, it is actually money that must be used to pay bills that come due later in the month. Inevitably, when that time comes they are short of cash.

To prevent this from happening to Persephone, I taught her the following simple principles for managing her cash flow. I urge you to share these with your children, and I assure you that you will save them and yourself significant heartaches in the future.

> *"I taught her the following simple principles for managing her cash flow."*

1. Create a realistic budget and stick to it.
2. Set up multiple bank accounts with online access and link them together.
3. Pay yourself weekly or biweekly. Wherever your money comes from, your employer, your parents or a school loan,

deposit your check in one of the online bank accounts; let's call it the master bank account.

4. Transfer 10% of your income from the master to a savings account.

5. Transfer the money intended to pay bills to a bill-paying account. Immediately transfer the equivalent of two weeks of expenses to this account.

For example, your rent is most probably due on the first of each month. If you are paid biweekly, transfer half the rent from the master account to the bill-paying account, and do the same with all your bills such as utilities, food, credit card payments, etc. If you are paid weekly, transfer a quarter of your monthly expenses to that account.

6. Pay all your bills by credit card whenever possible. Doing so causes you to write fewer checks and makes record-keeping simple and centralized.

7. Pay all your bills online. Program your accounts to automatically issue payments two days before the bills are due. This helps you in two very important ways:

   a. Your bills are always paid on time, and that is the most important ingredient for a good credit score.

   b. You avoid making the cardinal mistake of overspending and running short or "bouncing" a check. Consider this all too familiar example:

You have paid your bills with physical (paper) checks and mailed them to the intended payees on time and you feel good about it. The next day you check your account balance and discover that you have more money than you anticipated. To reward yourself, you decide to spend it on things you enjoy. A few days later the bank calls you with an "insufficient funds" message.

How could this happen? Here is how. When you pay by paper check, the money stays in your account until the check clears the bank, which, counting transit time and other factors, could take from a few days to a few weeks. Online bill payment removes the money from your account on the same day the check is issued, thus eliminating any unpleasant surprises. It is fast, secure, and automatic. It also saves you money because while many banks charge you for writing checks, most banks offer online bill payment for free.

8. Pay your credit card bills weekly. Programming your account to pay a quarter of your credit card bill each week reduces the finance charges assessed by the banks if you carry over balances from month to month. More important, you eliminate any risk of a late payment, and your credit score rises.

9. After you have followed steps 3 through 5, you should still have the money you budgeted for entertainment and the like.

10. Withdraw the full amount in cash. Use only cash for drinks with friends, dinners out, movies, etc. This is your safety valve. You can order only as many drinks as you have cash to pay for. Keep the credit card in your wallet and you will have no unpleasant surprises.

While saving money is important, establishing good credit is even more important. When Persephone was in high school, I got a joint credit card, which she shared with me. Initially I maintained control, and later supervised how she used it. As you might expect, she made some mistakes. When mismanagement or overspending was evident, I'd e-mail her a copy of the statement and ask her to justify specific expenses. Those were not happy days for her, but they provided a forum for accountability, discussion and education.

Knowingly or not, the entire time she was learning to control her spending, manage her cash flow, and establish some savings. Most important, she was also establishing credit. Persephone secured a full-time job before graduation, and a month later she asked to be cut off from any support on my part so that she could make herself financially independent. Soon thereafter, she was approved for an apartment lease within a day, instead of the expected week, and was told the expedited approval was due to her credit score.

A few weeks later, she was able to get a very nice car for herself entirely on her own creditworthiness. The following month she joined the ranks of American Express cardholders. Watching Persephone's ability to do these things as a young lady let me know that she was well on her way to independence.

Social Awareness

Many children who feel entitled to all the luxuries the world has to offer without a corresponding sense of gratitude will never become responsible adults. I always found it necessary to nurture social awareness in Persephone's younger years, to prevent her from becoming insulated in the relative comfort she was privileged to enjoy. Naturally, I wanted her to benefit from the best I could offer her, but I also wanted her to realize how blessed she was.

It was important to me to involve her in charity work on a consistent basis. I made sure she saw with her own eyes how many people had so much less than she could imagine. One year I collected the change I emptied from my pockets every day into a cigar box until it grew to a significant amount. Just before Thanksgiving I told her she could take it to the bank and keep 60 percent of it. When she asked where the rest would go, I told her, "You're going to donate it."

She was only 14 at the time, so of course I could see the disappointment on her face. Still, I told her that she could have that 60 percent only if she took the time to roll the remainder into change tubes and come with me to soup kitchens in Washington, D.C., to distribute the money. We drove through the area, and she rolled the window down and handed it out to homeless people who quickly gathered to accept it. She ended up handing out not 40 percent, but 60 percent of her money because it made her feel good. And as I detailed in the last chapter, she made this practice her own when she was in college and spearheaded the Hurricane Katrina relief effort.

How to Recognize Success

Success, particularly in parenting, is difficult to define. For the purposes of this book, I have defined it as raising a child to be a responsible and independent adult. Others might emphasize raising a happy adult, but I strongly believe a responsible and independent adult will be a much happier individual than a dependent and irresponsible one. But what about the maxim we hear so often to "pursue our dreams"? Where does that fit into the picture as we teach our kids to be grateful for what they have, be respectful and compassionate, be responsible and accountable for their decisions, and establish a good credit score?

Success as an adult lies between a dream and reality. You must dream big dreams, but you must also grasp reality well enough to make

CDO: CHIEF DADDY OFFICER

the right plans and maximize your chances of making your dreams a reality. And you must take action. I truly believe that if you have the same dream often enough, you must act on it and it will likely become a reality. Take no action, and it will be your everlasting nightmare.

I dreamed once of becoming a doctor, but learned enough about myself to realize that I enjoyed the business side of medicine more than the research or practicing side of it. I pursued that dream and have been able to achieve success at something I truly enjoy, while taking care of my family and myself.

"Take action. I truly believe that if you have the same dream often enough, you must act on it and it will likely become a reality. Take no action, and it will be your everlasting nightmare."

One of my greatest passions has always been flying. I came to America on a Boeing 747. It was my first flight ever, and my dream was to fly a plane myself one day. I did not change careers to become a pilot. I did not mortgage my house to buy a private jet. Instead, I took flying lessons in my spare time and gradually earned my pilot's license and advanced ratings. Not long ago, I bought a share of a plane as well. For me, it was the fulfillment of that dream.

Your son may love basketball, but he may not be good enough to play professionally. Why not encourage him to earn enough money doing something he also likes, which will allow him to play basketball on a regular basis in his spare time? Maybe he will even be able to build a gym, or coach his child's team. The same goes for many pursuits that make great hobbies but poor careers for all but the exceptionally talented.

The mantra in our culture is to try, try, try when it comes to your dreams, and this is in some ways good advice. No one should give up on something important too easily. But do you want your child to spend years pursuing a career with little to no success? Teach your child how to pursue a wise career choice he or she can enjoy, and to pursue other dreams along the way.

"Think of something you love doing, and then find a way to make a living at it and you'd never have to work a day in your life."

When my daughter was in middle school she asked me, "How will I know what I want to do for work when I grow up, and how will I know if I'd like it and be happy with it?" I repeated the exact words of one of my mentors, "Think of something you love doing, and then find a way to make a living at it and you'd never have to work a day in your life." She is well on her way to realizing her own dreams!

Priorities and Power

Adult life can feel overwhelming. Teach your children to separate what they can control from what they cannot. I had to approach my parenting adventure with Persephone knowing that I had no control over the past. There was no use dwelling on the nasty divorce her mother and I had gone through. Doing so would be nothing but wasted energy. I did, however, have significant control over our future, my attitude, my relationship with my daughter, and my company. I chose to focus on those things.

In my times of greatest stress and challenge, I concentrated my energy on taking care of my daughter and on growing my company the best way I knew how. I knew that these goals were largely under my control and that they were achievable. I tried my best not to waste energy on negative things such as self-pity or self-doubt, as they both are utterly incapacitating. Out of the disappointment of a failed marriage came a stable company and a flourishing relationship with my daughter on which I could build for the rest of my life.

Recently, while standing poolside enjoying good food, family and friends, I was asked how I'd like to be remembered. I smiled at the question, because it seemed more appropriate for a hospital visit than an afternoon barbeque. However, the answer I gave was no less true: "I want people to remember that I truly understood what it meant to be Persephone's father."

As of this writing, for nearly 24 years, I've been working at my most important job. So far, Persephone's life and our relationship bears out that it is a job well done. My business career has been and continues to be a wonderful ride. I am most indebted to it, because it has helped me be a better father.

Vacationing in Lewis Beach, Delaware. Summer of 1996.

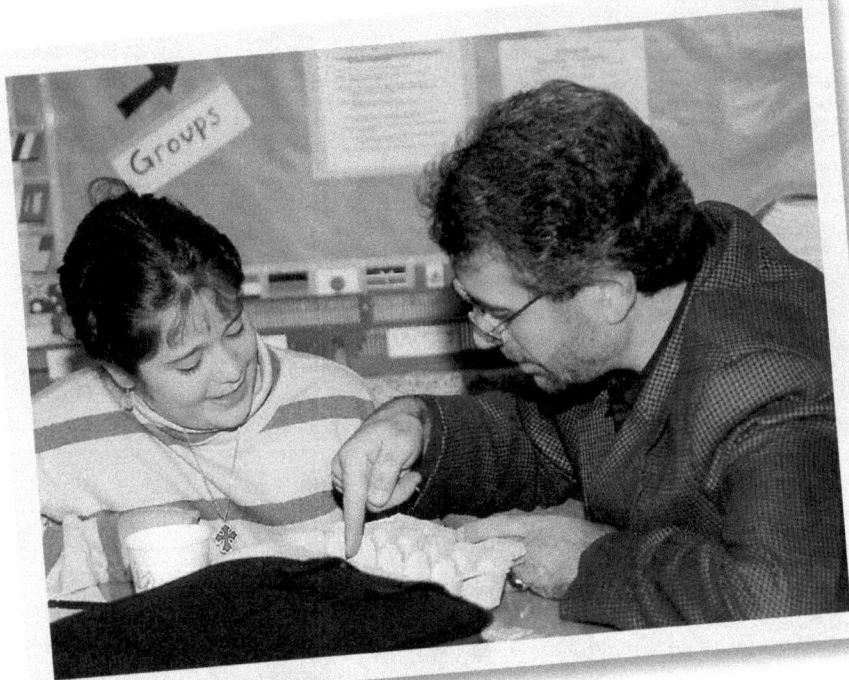

Fathers' Visiting Day at Persephone's School. November, 1996.

At my nephew's christening in Greece. June, 2003.

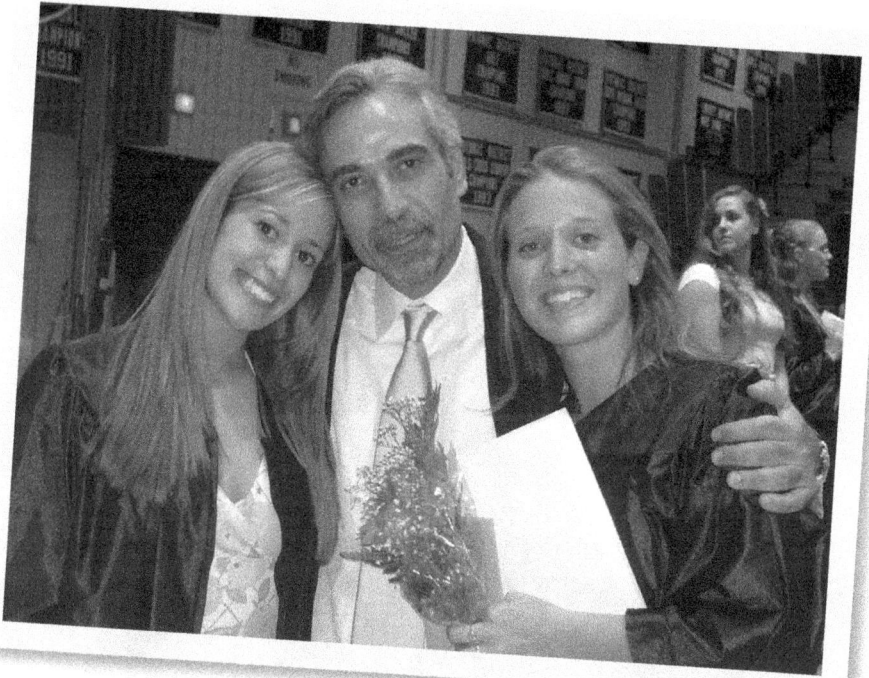

With Persephone and Tara at their High School graduation. June, 2005.

Tara and Persephone in my office. Tara's poem and *Fortune* in the background.
December, 2005.

Thanksgiving 2006.

Dancing with my daughter to "My way" at my 50th birthday celebration.
September, 2007.

On the eve of our wedding; from one beautiful daughter to four. Sarasota 2008.

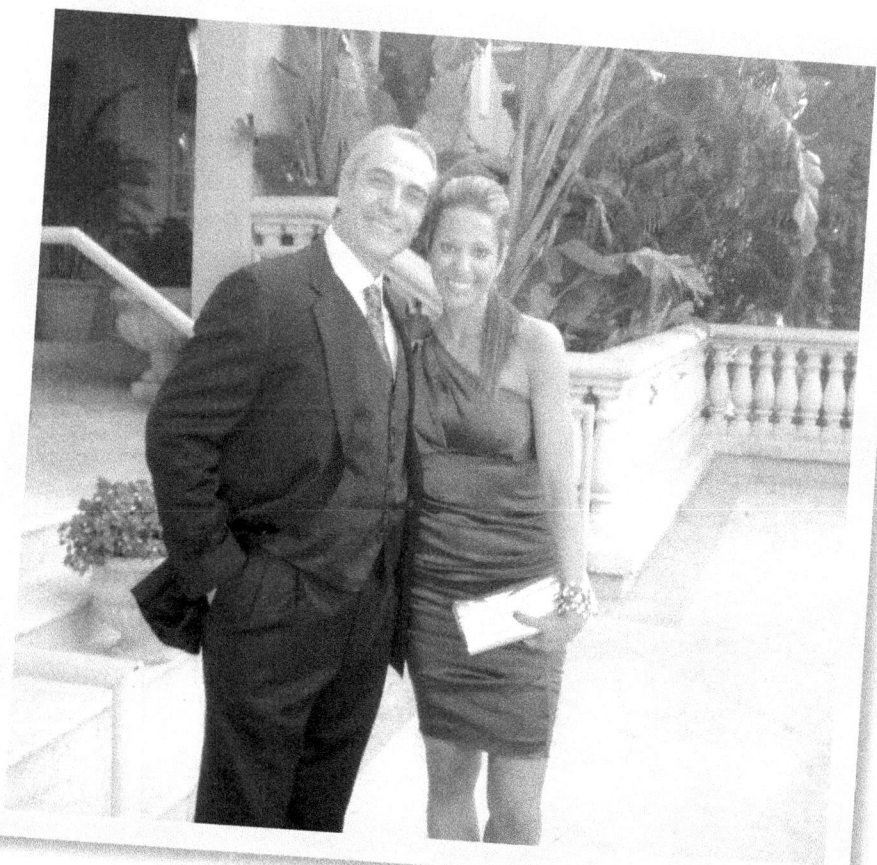

On my wedding day with Persephone. January, 2009.

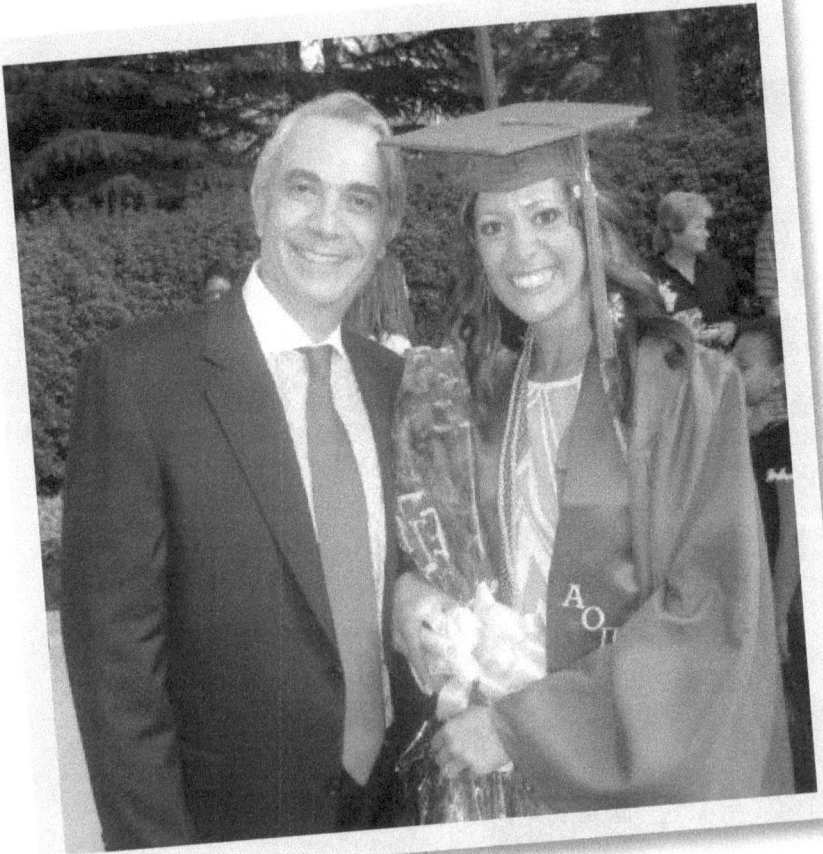

College graduation day. May, 2009.

Christmas 2010. With Juliana, Persephone, and her fiancé Eduardo.

There's two things I know for sure
She was sent here from heaven
And she's daddy's little girl
As I drop to my knees by her bed at night
She talks to Jesus and I close my eyes
And I thank God for all of the joy in my life
Oh but most of all

For butterfly kisses after bedtime prayer
Stickin' little white flowers all up in her hair
Walk beside the pony daddy it's my first ride
I know the cake looks funny daddy but I sure tried

Oh with all that I've done wrong
I must have done something right
To deserve a hug every mornin'
And butterfly kisses at night

Lyrics from ***Butterfly Kisses*** by Bob Carlisle

Epilogue

FOR YEARS, I COULD NOT SIT THROUGH the charming family movie *Father of the Bride.* Despite its warmth and humor, I would actually leave the room whenever it came on television. I suppose the story of a loving father who didn't want to face his daughter's impending marriage hit a little too close to home.

A lot has happened since the first printing of this book, and I wanted to update my readers on some new milestones in my CDO journey. On May 28, 2010, a young man named Eduardo met with Juliana and me to ask our blessing to marry Persephone. And as tempted as I was to behave like Steve Martin, I knew he was the one.

Two years of engagement and preparation flew by astonishingly fast. Everyone knows that the ladies plan the wedding, so I didn't expect to be consulted on much beyond the budget. Yet to my delight and shock, Persephone actually asked me to accompany her dress shopping!

"I am sure when you see the right dress, you'll know it," I assured her on a beautiful Saturday in August, as we strolled through midtown Manhattan.

She looked at me with her big brown eyes, squeezed my hand and answered, "Doodle, I'll know when I've found the right dress, because I'll see it on your face." And sure enough, there was one particular gown that brought us both to tears that afternoon. I still couldn't believe I was there to share the moment when she said yes to the dress.

A few weeks later she brought me a thank you gift. It was a linen handkerchief, embroidered with these words:

Doodle, you will always be the first man I ever loved.
Thank you for being there for me every step of the way.
Love, Persephone

On the morning of the big day, Persephone asked Juliana and me to join her for breakfast. The serene joy in her demeanor calmed the flurry of emotions in my soul. In typical Persephone-style, she thanked us for our support and gave us each a very thoughtful gift and a card.

Folded in the card was a copy of a letter she'd written for the Father's Day issue of a magazine. It was entitled "My Chief Daddy Officer." (A copy of this letter appears a few pages later.)

Before I could catch my breath, it was time. I have had many profound and meaningful experiences in my life, but none of them compared to that moment. As we walked down that aisle together, I felt like I was reliving every minute we had ever shared all at once. I kissed her and gave her hand to the man who moments later became her husband.

I had dreaded that moment for years, but now that it had arrived, it was perfect.

As I reflect back on that day, I am reminded that respect begets respect, honor begets honor, and sowing care, consideration and purpose into others - especially your child – will cause you to reap the same. You will find no better investment here on earth.

Then the moment came for the father of the bride to make his remarks to the new couple. This is what I said to them.

"Welcome to each and every one of you to My Big Fat Greco-Filipino Wedding...

Juliana and I, together with Ed and Mila, want to thank you all for joining us as we celebrate the marriage of our children Persephone and Eduardo. A special "Thank you" to those who have traveled from the Philippines, France and Greece to be with us today.

The love affair of Eddie and Persephone started a bit over four years ago. On May 27, 2008, (Memorial Day weekend) I met Eddie for the first time, and I was immediately impressed by four things about him:

- His footwear – white moccasins
- His hair style – a Mohawk
- His self-confidence which said, "I am totally comfortable in my own skin"
- And the way he looked at my Persephone

An appropriately emotional but highly composed Eddie asked to meet with Juliana and me to ask for our blessing to marry Persephone. This was two years ago, on Memorial Day weekend, May 28, 2010 at 6:27 pm .....and 23 seconds.

Two years later on Memorial Day weekend, today, they exchanged their vows. Coincidence, Fate, Kismet? You be the judge.

Persephone, there isn't a person in this room that does not know how I feel about you and what you mean to me, so as the father of the bride, I am breaking with tradition. And rather than talking to all of you about my daughter, I will talk to you about Eddie instead.

Thank you Eddie for becoming the President and Chief Cheer Leader of the "Persephone Fan Club" and screaming it from the rooftops. Thank you for your kind heart, generous soul, intuitive spirit, absolute selflessness, and your willingness to put Persephone's wellbeing ahead of almost anything else. Thank you for always being willing to do what is right, good, and nurturing to her soul. Thank you for always doing that without ever having to be asked.

Thank you for the respect, support and encouragement you show her in everything and anything she wants to do. Thank you, for being you.

Two years ago, when Eddie came to ask for our blessing to marry Persephone I told him that the right man to marry Persephone had not been born yet and probably never will be, but that he was as close to that man as I had ever seen walking this planet.

I was wrong.

That man had been born to Ed and Mila and was standing before me. That man is now my Persephone's husband and our son-in-law. That man, I am honored to call my friend.

Persephone and Eddie, as you begin a lifetime of togetherness my wish for you is to...

Never take the other for granted

Fuel the romance to continue through your lives

Always stand together facing the world.

Form a circle of love that Gathers-In the whole family.

Do not look for perfection in each other

Be flexible, patient, understanding.

Have the capacity to forgive and forget

Remember that Independence is Equal, Dependence is Mutual, and Obligation is Reciprocal

Remember to always have a sense of humor

You have married the right partner. Now continue your life together BEING the right partner.

And when you choose that the time is right, my wish for you is that you be blessed with children who are exactly like you.

I love you both."

Persephone gave me this letter the morning of her wedding. (She'd submitted it a week earlier for the Father's Day issue of a magazine.)

My Chief Daddy Officer

As a child, I never looked at my relationship with my Dad as "different" - I just knew it as unique and special. When I was 7 years old, my parents went through a tumultuous divorce resulting in my mother deciding to leave and move to Boston. Most kids by default would follow their mothers and though some may have had that same expectation for me; at the tender age of 9, I made a decision that one could say marked a pivotal point in both of our lives and paved the way for my relationship with my Dad being what it is today.

I made a choice - I wanted to live with my Dad full-time. As the CEO of his own pharmaceutical marketing company and now a single-Dad, he did not run away from the challenge, he ran towards it - he embraced it, cherished it and gave me a life and parent that some never get to experience.

I am a direct reflection of everything he has taught me and raised me to be and I'm proud of that fact. He has instilled values and life lessons in what would seem to be an obvious way, but what I've learned is not obvious to most. He showed me by example and then let me arrive at my own decisions (both good and bad). What I never grasped until later in life - he was always strategic and by that I mean he was always laying down the wireframe for an opportunity to teach me a life lesson. I always felt like he was 5 paces ahead of me (which when I was a teenager wasn't always fun); however, it always was for my benefit.

One of my favorite stories is when I was in high school and in the midst of college application time, I was struggling with what to do with my life (as most 17 year-olds will ponder.) At the time, I was dating someone who my Dad was less than fond of and who's lack of motivation was most worrisome to him. When I shared what my college aspirations were, which was to take a year off of school, work as a hostess at a local restaurant and reconsider in a year, he responded with "what a wonderful idea - minus the hostess job. In your year off you can apply to the Peace Corp or Americorp and build houses for those in need." What he was doing was letting me decide for myself, but giving me alternatives and guidelines so that this would benefit me; he allowed me the ability to lead myself to make the right decision for my career. Suffice it to say I submitted college applications the next day, because I realized Peace Corp equaled no blow-dryers.

It wasn't until my years in college when I realized that I was never missing anything in life - my Dad filled me with more love than a village of parents and provided me with a childhood and an adulthood serving as both Mom/Dad, confidant, best friend, designated driver, career advisor, relationship coach, fashion aficionado, just to name a few. My Dad is the businessman in a French-cuff shirt, who rolled up his sleeves to do his 7 year olds nails, the CEO that would pick up my calls during business meetings so he knew I was okay, and the father who without an iota of embarrassment in the inflection of his voice, would call asking for what kind of tampons I needed. When I reflected in my early college years, I recognized that most people didn't have one parent that behaved as lovingly and as selflessly as my Dad always treated me. There was never a time where my Dad wasn't present - he drove me to school in the mornings and tucked me in every night (which are still to this day some of my fondest memories.)

In the 24 years of my young life, he has always gone above and beyond to be physically and emotionally available to me and he's never missed any important (or non-important event). A few years ago, my Dad was traveling to Thailand for a huge meeting. Conveniently, my long-term boyfriend broke up with me. The person I always turned to was half way around the world, but it felt like no distance was between us. Despite the 12-hour time difference, he made himself available to talk to me, listen to me wail and cry and offer me his kind words to ease my heartache. It wasn't until I reached milestones in my own career that I could truly comprehend the magnitude of what he did. His emotional presence never dissipated as I got older - in fact in a lot of ways has increased. Throughout my two-year engagement, my fiancé and I would turn to my Dad for his input as far as color schemes, floral combinations and most importantly for my dress selection. He has delayed trips, rearranged schedules, all of which seemed effortless to me because he's never missed a beat.

I always noticed that my friends were drawn to my Dad for many of the same reasons I had taken for granted because he is all I knew - they too wanted a piece of his intellect, his astute business sense, his real-world wisdom. He is giving of his time, though he has little of it, to dedicate himself in helping my friends. He has employed two of them and has advised personally and professionally no less than 10 of my closest friends. He's helped prepare 5 others for job interviews - all of which were a great success.

It was at this time when the idea of my Dad writing a book begun. His book titled CDO Chief Daddy Officer, is his story on how he applied his business knowledge to the business of parenting. When the concept arose, he told me the only way he'd go through with it is if I was the co-contributor to the book. If at all possible, this has brought us even closer because it gave us a unique opportunity to work together and pull back the layers to the fundamentals of our relationship. The irony is that he wrote that book to discuss what he describes to be his crowning achievement - raising me - but what he doesn't know is that my proudest accomplishment is being just that - an accomplishment in his eyes.

Now, a week away from taking a walk down the aisle, I will have my number one man walking by my side. Though weddings usually represent "out with the old and in win the new," I am blessed to say that my soon-to-be husband is just receiving the passing of a baton from one man who I love to another. Because truthfully, nothing really has to change - our lives are just transitioning harmoniously together. Every day I cherish the blessing that I was born with, and I can only pray that as I turn a page in my life and start my own family that I will be half as great of a parent as he was - I will then feel that I succeeded.

Acknowledgments

THE EVENTS AND EXPERIENCES I have described throughout this book are relayed to the best of my recollection. My sole purpose in sharing them is to convey to the reader the challenges I faced and how I responded to them as a single father. My primary fact-checker was my daughter, but I am well aware that other people involved may have different memories or interpretations of these same events. By no means do I claim that mine is the only or the best interpretation.

Writing a book is a difficult endeavor for anyone, and I am thankful that I have not journeyed alone. I particularly wish to recognize the contributions of some of my fellow travelers. I am indebted my editorial consultant Julia Nelson and to my publicist Yolanda Harris for their numerous contributions to this project. I am grateful to our daughter Jessica Fox for her tireless editing efforts as well as her thoughtful comments and support. Thank you also to the entire team of Advantage Media Group, Inc.

I was fortunate to receive the professional counsel of Dr. Roxanna Wolfe in the review of the manuscript. Her direction and comments were invaluable to me and I sincerely thank her for her efforts and encouragement. I am also fortunate to have had the support and advice of Arthur Lafionatis, Esq. Once again, my friend, the road is better travelled with you on it, and I thank you for it. My early parenting was largely influenced by the wisdom of my dear friend George Kouroupas to whom I will forever be indebted. I'd also like to thank the members of my team at work, both past and present, for their efforts and loyalty over the years, and I apologize to all of those whose names should have been mentioned but did not make this list.

Of course I would like to thank Persephone. This book is after all about my life with you, and most of its contents were lived by the two of us together. I am astonished by your recollection of detail, as well as the depth of your contributions, encouragement and support throughout this emotional journey. Above all, I thank you for giving me an unexpected gift; I did not think it was possible for us to get any closer, but through this trip down memory lane we achieved exactly that.

I am a lucky man indeed. I am proud to be your father and I thank you for allowing me to be your dad. May you be blessed with a daughter like you! I love you so.

To my wife, Juliana, in the words of Jerry Maguire, "You complete me." You are my friend, confidant, soul mate, and mother to our daughters. You will always be my muse and I love you for it.

You've done well in business but not at home?

You can run your household just fine but are afraid to enter today's workforce?

Learn how you can transfer the skills you already have and apply them with equal efficiency in the workroom and the family room.

1. Visit us at **www.ChrisEfessiou.com** and join our group of parents and professionals who are getting critical information on both business and personal relationships.

2. Listen to *Straight Up With Chris: Real Talk on Business and Parenthood* on Voice America Radio, as leading business and parenting experts share unique insights into today's world of working parents. **www.StraightUpWithChris.com**

3. Book Chris to speak with your group on a variety of topics, including *The Art of Negotiation, Living the Leadership Role, Creating a Family Culture at Work and at Home, Adopting Business Principles for Family Success*, and *Finding the Common Solution*. **www.chrisefessiou.com/speaking**

4. Tap into Chris' extensive range of knowledge including negotiation skills, marketing strategies, team building, employee engagement, and defining and cultivating individual leadership skills to ensure a competitive advantage for your company.

Transferring business skills to personal relationships

Please contact us at **info@ChrisEfessiou.com** or
visit **www.ChrisEfessiou.com**

About the Author

Entrepreneur, Marketing Strategist, Negotiations Architect, Speaker, Radio Show Host and Author of *CDO® Chief Daddy Officer®: The Business of Fatherhood*, Chris Efessiou understands first hand that the dynamics of success are the same whether you're standing at the front of a conference room or tucking your child into bed at night. Through his own personal experiences, Chris Efessiou – founder and CEO of SRxA Strategic Pharmaceutical Advisors – shares his discovery of how skills critical to becoming a successful business leader can be seamlessly applied with equal efficiency to both parenting and personal relationships.

In the last 27 years, Chris has been at the heart of the strategic introduction of more than 20 new products in the global pharmaceutical marketplace and engineered the turnaround of several others. In 2005 he engineered professional communications and education campaigns which helped a virtually unknown OTC product become a billion dollar brand, and in 2011 he engineered MAAX™, a hybrid marketing vehicle, which produced the largest known Return on Investment in the industry.

While building his first company, he found himself raising his then seven year old daughter as a single dad by applying his business knowledge to the art of parenting. Planning, setting expectations and measuring results, building team unity and empowerment, fostering bilateral communication, mentoring, leading by example, and being physically present and emotionally available are essential components for both a prosperous business and loving family.

Chris is the host of *Straight Up with Chris: Real Talk on Business and Parenthood*, accessing more than 4 million listeners each month as one of Voice America's top radio shows. The show features in-depth interviews with top business leaders, parenting experts and other intriguing guests who share their experiences and advise the audiences. Recent guests have included Ken Blanchard best-selling author of the *One Minute Manager*, retired FBI Profiler Dr. Mary Ellen O'Toole, and NBC family expert Dr. Michele Borba.

www.ingramcontent.com/pod-product-compliance
Lightning Source LLC
Chambersburg PA
CBHW060656150426

42813CB00070B/3417/J